In Heaven!

Moments in Heaven Series

Book 1

But even if we, or an angel from heaven, preach any other gospel to you than what we have preached to you, let him be accursed.

—GAL 1:8

In Heaven!

DEAN BRAXTON

In Heaven! by Dean Braxton
Printed in the United States of America

3rd Edition
ISBN 978-0-9978372-7-8

www.Deanbraxton.com

Dedicated to my children

Constance, Anthony, Marsha, Michael, Tiffany and Gabriel

Contents

Foreword

There are a lot of things written about Heaven in the Bible, but God's people haven't understood them because the true meaning was hidden within its words. Once you have read this book, many of your questions will have been answered as mine were. I have been serving the Lord for well over 60 years and have always had a hunger to know what Heaven is really like. God brought Dean and Marilyn Braxton into my life to give me a firsthand view of what it's like.

It was in 2007 that I met Dean at a Friday night Bible Study where he had been invited to share his experience of dying, going to Heaven, and then coming back. Marilyn shared her side of the struggles that she faced at Dean's side at the hospital, and Dean shared about Heaven. The first thing he found out was that his spirit instantly knew where to go. Thank God our citizenship is in Heaven! We go Home!

Shortly after that, Pastor Butler invited Dean and Marilyn to come to our church and share their testimony and because of that pastor, Dean and I have spent many hours talking about his experience and how it fits the Word of God. What a wonderful and glorious life we have ahead of us!

While Dean was in Heaven for an hour and forty-five minutes, the Lord showed him many things and downloaded into his spirit so much information that two things happened. One was that he didn't want to come back to the earth. Who would? The other was that he knew he needed to verify everything he saw there in the Word of God.

So my friend, as you read this book you will be encouraged, blessed, and strengthened to be "strong in the Lord and in the power of His might." I trust that this book will also encourage you to become a soul winner. The signs we see all around us tell us that our Lord is coming back soon.

Our brother in Christ,

John Cook, Assistant Pastor
By His Word Christian Center—Tacoma, WA

Introduction

Over the years, I've never been impressed with heavenly experiences in people's lives because I could never really validate them with the Word of God. About two years ago, my assistant in the ministry introduced me to Dean Braxton and his experience of going to Heaven. This time my spirit bore witness with his testimony, and so the Lord spoke to me about having him come and share with our church. From that moment on, Dean and his lovely wife, Marilyn, have remained with us ever since.

I really feel blessed having Dean and the revelation of his experience in my life. The tremendous witness of so many scriptures to his description of Heaven, even to the point of revealing the understanding of passages that we never had the insight into before, was life-changing. So take the journey with Dean as he connects scripture to every account of his experience and be blessed!

Jann T. Butler, Senior Pastor
By His Word Christian Center—Tacoma, WA

(Sentences that have a * following them have scripture support given in the chapter notes at the back of the book.)

Chapter 1

"No, It Is Not Your Time"

What do I remember of the first time I was before Jesus? I remember He said, "No, It is not your time. Go back."* I seemed to be OK with that. So I left to come back to earth. I got to what I would call the edge of Heaven, and knew that my body on earth was not ready for me to return to it. I cannot tell you how or why I knew, I just knew. While returning back to the feet of Jesus, I saw a lot of different things throughout Heaven. I also communicated with a number of beings. I call them BEINGS because they we're BEING everything God had created them to be.

When I reached Jesus the second time, He again said, "No, It is not your time. Go back." The second time He told me to go back, His voice was a little more firm, and it seem like I cried on the inside. So I left again. When I reached the edge of Heaven this time, I experienced something that does not bring happiness.

At the edge of Heaven is thick darkness—blackness such as you will never experience here on earth.* You could hold it in your hands if you wanted to. I do not think our physical body could penetrate it. It was that thick. I had to pass through this darkness to get to Heaven, and later, when I left Heaven to return back to earth, I passed through it again. I knew it was filled with demons. But, I also knew that when I passed through this blackness, no demon could touch me because I was a child of God. I did not experience any fear going through it to Heaven, or when I left to come back to earth.

This second time I reached the edge of Heaven, I heard the cries of those who were in Hell.* I heard the screams, the shrieks, the screeches, the squeals, and the yells of pain from the fallen creations (people) of God. I knew if I looked over this edge, I would see what was happening to them there. But I just did not have any desire to look. It was not Jesus's will for any human to be there. Since it was not His will, it was also not His will I look. Thinking about this always brings great sadness to me.

Again, I traveled through parts of Heaven and communicated with more of God's creations as I returned to Jesus's feet. When I came before Him the third time, He said again, "NO, IT IS NOT YOUR TIME. GO BACK!" He was really stern with me, and again it seem like I was crying on the inside, but this time it was like I was crying like a baby on the inside. These are the only words He spoke to me. The other way He communicated with me was almost the same way a computer receives information. He would just look at me and put information into me that He wanted me to know. I remember looking into His eyes as He downloaded all kinds of information into me. I continue to experience and acquire new information and insights even now. I am discovering new ways to explain what I saw. I understand things in the Holy Bible as I have never understood them before. Even as I am writing this, there are new revelations that I will put in this explanation of what happened to me.

The Pain In My Side

At the time this happened, I was the Program Manager for two King County Superior Juvenile Courts in Seattle, Washington. One court works with juveniles who are chemically dependent (Drug Court), and the other works with juveniles that are mentally ill (Treatment Court). This day just happened to be my Drug Court day. On mornings before a court hearing, a team of professionals would discuss the youths appearing before the court that day to determine how they are doing. On the team is a judge, the judge's bailiff, a staff member from detention, a prosecuting attorney, a defense attorney, a police officer, an educator, a mental health counselor, a chemical dependency counselor, two juvenile probation counselors, and myself, the manager.

On Thursday, May 4th, 2006, I was driving to work, knowing that the pain in my side was not going away as easily as it had in the past. But, I believed if I could get to work and lay on the floor, the pain would go away. When I arrived at work at 7 AM, I went to the bathroom. I thought the pain would go away after I relieved myself, but it did not. I lay on the floor, and still, the pain did not relent. This time, I knew the pain would not go away. I had had this pain before, and I knew it was kidney stones. I was thinking that if I would pass them, the pain would stop. However, this time, something was wrong.

I decided that I needed to go back home. I left the building and informed the security guard at the entry door that I was heading home, and asked him if he would let my staff know I was leaving. He said he would. When he asked me what was wrong, I told him, "Kidney stones". I also said I would be OK. Out in the parking lot, I ran into a co-worker and asked her to take the snacks to the staff meeting before court because I was leaving.

On My Way to the Hospital

The drive back home was 45 minutes to an hour. On the way home, I vomited a number of times in the car. When I finally arrived home, I was still in a lot of pain, and so I lay down on the hard floor again, hoping this would relieve the pain, but it did not. I decided to go to the emergency room (ER). When I entered the ER at the hospital, I was doubled over and I let the staff know I believed I was in pain because of kidney stones. They took me right into a room and gave me some pain medication. I was not used to taking medications. In fact, I could not remember taking any sick days in the past three years. My wife, Marilyn, showed up and talked with the doctor about the problem. The doctor confirmed that I had numerous kidney stones with one stuck high on the right side and it was the one causing all of my problems. The doctor decided to operate the next day and wanted me to stay overnight.

With most kidney stones the doctor will use a machine that employs ultrasonic waves (ultra sound) to break the stones up so the patient can pass them easier. It just so happened that this machine would be at that hospital the next day. He wanted me to stay in the hospital overnight and to have the stones broken up, using this machine the next day.

A Simple Operation

Marilyn had to deal with not only me being in the hospital, but another family situation that needed her attention. We were supposed to leave that night to visit family in Texas, and then return with our son, Gabriel, who was attending Christ for the Nations Bible College. Marilyn and a friend were able to get our flight changed from that evening to May 8th. So, everything was set. It was supposed to be a simple operation, and I would be out the next day. That is what I believed would happen because I had this same operation four years ago. I checked in one morning and I was out that afternoon.

Seven days later, I came to in the Intensive Care Unit (ICU) at another hospital, and I was wondering, "What happened?" (Later, in this book my wife will give you her account of what happened during that time.) All I can remember is that after the operation, the doctors and nurses were trying to give me oxygen, but I could not breathe. Then, they wanted to put a pic-line in me so I signed a paper to OK the procedure.

When they took the breathing tube out of my mouth, I looked at my parents and older brother and told them I had seen Jesus three times. I knew I had died and was prayed back to life by many people who believed Jesus would heal me. Later, I found out that the hospital staff did CPR on me for an hour and 45 minutes. How long was I with Jesus? I cannot tell you. It seemed long, and it seemed short. I know EVERYTHING IS RIGHT, where Jesus is, and THERE IS NOTHING WRONG!* Some say it is peaceful, but it far exceeds peace because there is nothing to be peaceful from.* When I first arrived in Heaven and knelt before Jesus, all I could do, was say, "YOU DID THIS FOR ME?!! THANK YOU, THANK YOU, THANK YOU, THANK YOU, THANK YOU, and THANK YOU!!"* I could have said this for the next 3000 years or more, and I still would have wanted to keep going. Jesus is bright, and we who are RIGHT with Him can look at Him. He is brighter than the noonday sun, but we can still look at Him, if we are RIGHT with Him. There is more to tell, but that will have to wait for now. All I can end with now is that: EVERYTHING WAS RIGHT!!

Chapter 2

I Am Just a Man

Before we go any further in this book I want everyone to know that I am just a man. I was not sent back with any super hero powers. I have the same Holy Spirit in me that each one of us who have asked Jesus to be their Lord and Savior has within. Some people have tried to treat me as if I were special because of what happened to me. I've even heard others say I was lucky or blessed to go to Heaven and come back because I was able to see Jesus and God, the Father. I must let everyone know that I was sent back to do the same thing that all of us that accept Jesus into our lives as Lord and Savior are supposed to do.* God commissioned all of us to tell people about Jesus and to share with them how very much He loves them. I am no different than anyone else who loves Jesus.

Let's look at the story about a man named Thomas in the book of John.

JOHN 20:24-29 (NKJV)

"Now Thomas, called the Twin, one of the twelve, was not with them when Jesus came. The other disciples therefore said to him, "We have seen the Lord." So he said to them, "Unless I see in His hands the print of the nails, and put my finger into the print of the nails, and put my hand into His

> side, I will not believe." And after eight days His disciples were again inside, and Thomas with them. Jesus came, the doors being shut, and stood in the midst, and said, "Peace to you!" Then He said to Thomas, "Reach your finger here, and look at My hands; and reach your hand here, and put it into My side. Do not be unbelieving, but believing." And Thomas answered and said to Him, "My Lord and my God!" Jesus said to him, "Thomas, because you have seen Me, you have believed. Blessed are those who have not seen and yet have believed."

Thomas believed AFTER he saw Jesus, and Jesus said to him, "Thomas, because you have seen me, you have believed. Blessed are those who have not seen and yet have believed."

Everyone who has NOT seen Jesus as I have seen Him is blessed because Jesus said so. If you that know Jesus as Lord and Savior, you are blessed, blessed, and blessed. We all have the same job to accomplish here on earth and that is to tell as many people as we can about our Lord and Savior, Jesus Christ.

What Really Matters Is That You Are There!

If you do not believe me or my experiences in Heaven, that is OK. The most important thing is that you do go to Heaven. When you get there you will see Heaven for yourself. It won't even matter if I am right. What will matter is that you are there!*

I have come to understand that it really is not me who gets a person into Heaven or keeps them out. It really is not anyone here on earth. It is Jesus. It is all about Him, and because of that understanding, I do not have to perform to get into Heaven, and you do not have to perform either.* A person who is approved of God will want to serve Him because they love Him, not for what it will get them.

They will proclaim His name to all and will walk in His ways because of the love they have for Him.

So again, if after reading this book, you have a hard time believing what I have written, that is OK. Many of the things I write about won't get you in or keep you out of Heaven. Many of the different beliefs that separate the church denominations will not affect whether you go to Heaven or not. I do believe some of those beliefs may stop you from being a more effective witness for Jesus, but they will not keep you from entering Heaven. Jesus is looking at your heart. There are many people in Heaven whom I did not think would make it, but did, and many whom I believed would make it, but did not. Jesus knows the heart of a person.* All I can say is that when He looked at me, He saw Himself, and I was accepted into Heaven.*

Chapter 3

Everything is Right
"You Did This for Me?!!"

When the doctor first took the breathing tube out of my mouth, I looked up at the person who was sitting by my bed and singing a song about Jesus. It was Anthony, a friend, whose job at the hospital was to help with the breathing machines. He and his wife, Monique, had become good friends since we had met in February. So, when I took that first big breath, it was like coming out of water. I knew I had died. I looked at Anthony, and I said, "Anthony, I have seen Jesus! You need to go tell Monique and your church. You do not have to hope there is a Jesus. He is real. I have seen him!" All I could hear him say in a deep voice was, "Yeah." I saw a big smile on his face, with maybe a tear or two, every time I repeated myself, "I saw Jesus!" I told him over and over.

Something Must Have Really Gone Wrong!

Later, my family came into the room. Up until that time, I had not really known what had happened that had caused me to die. So, when I saw my parents come through the curtain in ICU, I said to myself, "Something must have really gone wrong!" I knew that the doctors would not call in family, unless the patient were dying or had died.

My parents live in a little town called Atwater in California, and I had remembered they had been out of town, visiting my mother's sister in Texas. I knew they had come a long way to see me. When they came through those curtains I knew I had been in big trouble. When my oldest brother came through those curtains, I knew something had really gone wrong! He also lived in California.

My mother came to the left side of the bed, my dad stopped at the foot of the bed, and my brother came to the right side of the bed. I looked at my mother and said, "Mom, I have seen Jesus three times. The first time He said, "No, it is not your time. Go back." Jesus said the second time, "No, it is not your time. Go back." Then I said to my mother, "Jesus said to me a third time, "NO, IT IS NOT YOUR TIME. GO BACK!" and I told them I cried. They just smiled as I told them what I saw. I also had a word for each of them from Jesus. I cannot tell you what He had me share with them. They are the only ones whom I can tell what Jesus said to them. I told them the story of seeing Jesus three times, and His telling me that it was not my time and to go back, over and over.

Thank You, Thank You, Thank You....

Again, I repeat that I know everything is RIGHT where Jesus is and there is nothing wrong.* Some say it is peaceful, but it far exceeds peace because there is nothing to be peaceful from in Heaven.* When I first stood before Jesus, all I could do was say, "YOU DID THIS FOR ME?!! THANK YOU, THANK YOU, THANK YOU, THANK YOU, THANK YOU, AND THANK YOU!"* I could have said this for the next 3000 years or more, and still, I would have wanted to keep going.

Jesus is bright and we that are RIGHT with Him can look at Him. He is brighter than our sun, but we can still look at him. There is nothing wrong everything is RIGHT! When I say everything is RIGHT,

I mean, everything is RIGHT! We seem to think here on earth that everything is peaceful there with Jesus. We are right in the sense that we desire peace from the pain that is in this world now.

JOHN 14:1-6 (NKJV)

> "Let not your heart be troubled; you believe in God, believe also in Me. In My Father's house are many mansions; if it were not so, I would have told you. I go to prepare a place for you. And if I go and prepare a place for you, I will come again and receive you to Myself; that where I am, there you may be also. And where I go you know, and the way you know." Thomas said to Him, "Lord, we do not know where You are going, and how can we know the way?" Jesus said to him, "I am the way, the truth, and the life. No one (*the Greek word is "oo-dice" meaning nothing*) comes to the Father except through Me."

When I first got to Heaven, all I wanted to do or could do was praise Jesus.* It seemed to me that I already knew what to do. No one had to tell me. I just knew what to do. I knew that we praise Jesus and Father God, no one else.* The only ones who receive praise are the Father and Jesus in Heaven. They are THE ONLY ONES.*

Where Was the Holy Spirit?

I need to stop and say right here, that I did not mention the Holy Spirit because His main work is here on earth. It is not that He is not there. After all, Jesus told His followers through His Word that the Holy Spirit will be with them always.

JOHN 16:14 (NKJV)

"And I (Jesus) will pray the Father, and He will give you another Helper, that He may abide with you forever."

So I had the Holy Spirit abiding with me in Heaven, and He was still abiding inside of me. I have said this many times to people. If we, who know Jesus as Lord and Savior, only understood whom we have within us! We have the FULLNESS of God inside of us. Someday that may be the subject of another book.

Praising Him Was All I Needed

Everything within me praised Him.* Everything I was made of cried out in praise to Jesus. Not my body, of course, since it had stayed here on earth, but my spirit and my soul, the real me, worshipped, with my whole being.*

I tell people, sometimes, that if I had had 10,000 mouths, they all would have been praising the Father and Jesus at this time. During this praising, it seemed like I was turning into God's LOVE.* I felt pure JOY. It seemed to me that I could live off the praising.* I did not need any food. Praising Him seemed to be all that I needed.* He had met all my needs. I say that because everything was right. Everything was right with me, right with every living being around me, and right with my relationship with God.

When you are there in Heaven with Jesus you are not thinking about what you left here on earth. You are thinking about what He did for you to make Heaven possible. Then I said, "You did this for me!

Thank you, thank you, and thank you," I was thinking of how He died on the cross for me and because of that action, I was there with Him. Not because of what I did, but what He did for me when I accepted Him as my Lord and Savior.*

I Saw Jesus on the Cross

I remember looking up to Jesus and seeing Him hanging on the cross for me. He was not really hanging on the cross, but somehow at that moment I could see Him hanging on the cross within my thinking. I knew that what He did on the cross was for me.* I knew that I knew.* The only reason I was in Heaven with Him was because of what He had done for me, and I knew it. I knew I was complete and perfect because of what He had done.* I knew He saw Himself in me and I was allowed into Heaven.* I knew that none of my works had done this. It was all His works, even the good works I had done was His working through me.* It seemed like Heaven was made just for me. I knew it was for others also, but right then, it just seemed as if it had been made only for me.*

My Place, My Space

I came to really understand what Jesus intended when He said "I go to prepare a place for you" (John 14:2). I knew I was in my place and that no one could take my place.* Jesus loved me so much that He made a place just for me and no one else could take that place or my space.

JOHN 14:2 (NKJV)

> "In My Father's house are many mansions; *(mansions literally means dwellings place, a stopping place or resting-place)* if it were not so, I would have told you. I go to prepare a place for you." {*Place: Greek: topos, Definition: 1) place, any portion or space marked off, as it were from surrounding space 1a) an inhabited place, as a city, village, district 1b) a place (passage) in a book, 2a) the condition or station held by one in any company or assembly 2b) opportunity, power, occasion for acting. a spot (general in space, but limited by occupancy)*}

I Had No Memory of Sin

Another reason I said "You did this for me," is because I felt as if I had never sinned in my whole life.* I knew I had been set free from true death (sin), and it could not keep me from Jesus and the Father.* I had no remembrance of sinning at all,* and I knew Jesus could not have reminded me, for I was forgiven and He did not remember any of my sins.* Again I knew that I knew that I knew!*

I know I did not want to leave such a place! It was not that I did not love my wife, children, other family members, or friends. It was because everything was just right in Heaven, as I said before. I knew I could never be separated from my Father and Jesus,* and I came to understand that true death is being separated from God.* I also came to realize that no one could hurt me in this place.*

Chapter 4

Pressing In

Marilyn, my wife, currently works with the elderly, as an Activity Assistant. She has worked in the medical field for the past 34 years in a number of positions: Certified Nurse's Aide, Endoscopy Technician, Adult Family Home Manager, Physical Therapy Aide and Home Health Care Aide. At the time of this incident she worked with an organization that contracted her out to work in local hospitals and nursing homes. She is the one who led the charge of praying me back to life on this earth. I call her the "General of Prayer". You are about to read her account of what she went through and how she battled to get me back on this earth. In her story are 10 biblical keys to winning a battle with the devil and his army of demons. Obviously, she won this one!

Marilyn's Testimony

Thursday, May 4th—I discovered that Dean was in the St. Francis Hospital Emergency Room at 12 noon after I checked my voice mail. One of the nurses had left a message telling me that I needed to pick Dean up and take him home. I was working at another hospital and, so I told the nurse there that I needed to leave. When I got to the hospital, Dean was asleep from the pain medication they had given him. The Emergency Room doctor told me that Dean had kidney stones and a kidney infection. The stone that was located high up on his right side was the one that was causing the most pain. The doctor suggested that Dean stay overnight in order to get IV antibiotics and fluids. Dean was in-and-out of this conversation due to the sedation caused by the pain medication.

Later that evening, the urologist or kidney specialist came to the room to talk with Dean and me. He told us that it would be a good idea to have the kidney stones blasted by ultra sound on Friday morning and then Dean would not have to endure all the pain. We agreed, thinking that Dean would be home the next day. When I left the hospital that evening, Dean had a fever, was having chills, and he was sleeping off and on.

Friday Morning, May 5th—Dean is still not aware of much due to the medication they were giving him and to a fever of 104. The doctor planned to go ahead with the surgery, anyways. When we went into the surgery waiting area to get questions answered that we might have had, Dean asked if the process was over, when he had not even gone into the operating room yet.

After the surgery, Dean was in recovery for almost three hours. I was able to spend the last half hour with him in the recovery room. It was at this time that the doctor who had administered Dean's pain medicine while he was in surgery came into the room. He told me that Dean had a very bad infection and he needed to go to the Intensive Care Unit (ICU) to receive fluids, more antibiotics, and to be observed. I was able to talk with my husband while he was in recovery. He was complaining about the oxygen mask being uncomfortable, and so, the nurses changed it for him. Dean was also attached to several different IV pumps in his arm.

After Dean was moved to the ICU, the doctor there told both of us that they wanted to put a PICC line in Dean's neck so that they could take away some of the IV lines in his arm. A PICC line would make it easier if they needed to draw blood for tests. Dean understood that this was going to happen. I left as they started this procedure.

I returned to the room, after being summoned by the nurse. The PICC line was already in, but in Dean's chest, not his neck. I looked at my husband and could see that he was hardly breathing and that his lips looked ashy or gray. I asked what happened and the doctor told me that he reached a blockage in Dean's neck. I was told that they needed to intubate, to put a tube down Dean's throat, immediately, or else he could die.

At that time we lived about five minutes from the hospital, so as they began this procedure, I left in order to pick up some things. I was praying on the way, of course, and as I drove onto the street, the surgeon called me on my cell phone to tell me my husband had coded. His heart had stopped. They were doing CPR (Cardiopulmonary Resuscitation). All I could say was, "What?!"

I called our son and daughter, Gabriel and Tiffany, who were away at college, to tell them to pray for their dad. I continued home, praying more intensely, and calling others asking them to pray also. I called a friend who was on her way to the hospital and she said she would come by to pick me up.

Key 1: *Marilyn first reached out to those she believed would stop and pray. I needed prayer, she needed prayer, and the doctors needed prayer. Later in this book I will tell you about those prayers. I saw them as I was going to Heaven and as I was coming back from Heaven.*

When my friend and I returned to the hospital, we did not see Dean right away because the doctors were still working on him. I called Dean's parents who had been visiting relatives in Texas. They had to return to California prior to coming to Washington. They talked with the doctor and came as fast as they could. The doctors worked on Dean for 1 hour and 45 minutes. It was during this time that many friends showed up in the waiting area and we prayed together in faith for Dean. After we prayed, I felt compelled to sing a song of praise and to glorify the Lord.

Key 2: *In the midst of the storm Marilyn praised God. She started to press into God and not run away from Him.*

The doctor told me how touch-and-go things were with Dean. He was doing all that he could do for Dean, and would know more in the morning. Now was the time for prayer and trusting God. I knew that Dean was being prayed for by many people in many places throughout the world. Those of us at the hospital now joined this chorus of declarations, praises, and thanksgiving. We did not demand that God do something, we did not beg Him, but we asked the Father in Jesus's name for healing. We thanked the Lord God that Dean was healed by the stripes of Jesus according to His Word. I refused to entertain doubt, but instead I trusted the Word of God for His promises concerning Dean's life.

I knew I had access to the throne of grace and that I could go boldly as a child of the Most High. Not only did I ask, but I thanked the Lord for what He was doing in Dean, even though the circumstances looked bad. I purposed in my heart to not blame God, for the Word says it is the devil that comes to steal, kill, and destroy. Jesus comes to give abundant life (John 10:10) and I claimed that life for my husband."

JOHN 10:10 (NKJV)

"The thief does not come except to steal, and to kill, and to destroy. I (Jesus) have come that they may have life, and that they may have it more abundantly."

Key 3: *Marilyn had a close walk with God before this incident happened. She was reading her Bible and praying on a continual basis. She knew what the Bible said about this situation. She knew that Jesus came to give abundant life and that Satan came to steal, kill, and destroy. She went to battle knowing what her God came to do for me. He came to give abundant life and at that time I was not living that life.*

This situation I was facing was all so crazy and so sudden. At times it almost felt unreal and dream-like, a nightmare for sure. Dean had been fine this morning. Yes, he had been in pain from the kidney stones, but now a few hours later, he was fighting for his life. His body was already filling up with the fluids from all the IVs that were being pumped into him. He was now on several medications, including insulin. I felt the need to go home and PRAY. I knew I needed to battle the enemy for I did not know what the rest of the night or the coming days would bring.

When I arrived home, I cried. I thanked the Lord for what a good husband Dean had been. He had put up with me. I thanked the Lord that Dean had been a good father to our children. I released the angels of God to be encamped roundabout Dean. I believe there is power in the shed blood of Jesus, and I covered Dean continually in that blood. Needless to say, I did not get much sleep that night, and the next morning, I found myself on the floor, still praying in the spirit. I would do this for the next three mornings.

Saturday Morning, May 6th—Because Dean's blood sugar count was 500 and a normal one would be much lower, I was told that he needed to be transferred to a different hospital, Tacoma General, to be on kidney dialysis continually. His kidneys had not functioned at all during the night, and so now, his body was going into septic shock. Dean's body was very swollen from the fluids. He was on 100% ventilation which meant a machine was doing the breathing for him. Dean was taken by ambulance that day with a nurse to care for him and all of the apparatus that he was hooked up to.

Later, I found out that even through this relocation, the Lord was watching over Dean. Dean was to be transferred to a different hospital. Most of the time a patient coming from St. Francis would go to the bigger local sister hospital, St. Joseph Hospital in Tacoma. Dean instead was transferred to Tacoma General Hospital. When I was talking to the supervisor of the nurses that was in charge that day, I found out why. Because I had worked at Tacoma General before, I knew her. She was very surprised that Dean was my husband and was very glad that she had chosen to take him at Tacoma General Hospital.

She said that when she got the call that day to take a crucially ill patient from St. Francis Hospital, she knew she should. So, as the nursing supervisor, she accepted Dean as a patient and when asked by the charge nurse why she was doing it, she said, "I don't know, but I just felt that we should." The Lord is so good!

Dean had a very good nurse on duty that morning. The nurse was very positive, and I knew that she and I would get along just fine. Dean was hooked up to dialysis right away. He just laid there without a clue as to what was going on. Many people came to pray for him and many others made themselves available to me if I needed anything. I refused to accept a negative report. I did not deny there were negative reports, but I refused to accept them, and refused to let those reports be the final answer. I chose to believe the report of the Lord. One doctor told me it could be a long time before Dean would be back to himself, and there could be the possibility of brain damage. I told him that it did not have to be a long time.

Key 4: *Marilyn heard what the doctor said to her, and did not argue with him about his diagnosis, but she kept her mind on what the Bible said. The doctors were doing the best they could, but Marilyn knew that Jesus could do better. So she stuck with what Jesus said.*

When I got home that night, I prayed for Dean long, hard, and loud. I told the devil who comes to steal, kill and destroy to take his hands off my husband. My body felt as if it were on fire as sweat dripped onto my nightshirt. My shirt became so wet that I took it off and laid it on a chair. I took the shirt with me to the hospital the Next morning and laid it on Dean's head.

ACTS 19:11-12 (NKJV)

"Now God worked unusual miracles by the hands of Paul, so that even handkerchiefs or aprons were brought from his body to the sick, and the diseases left them and the evil spirits went out of them."

Key 5: *Marilyn was acting on what she had read that Paul had done in the Bible. She knew the power of God was on her the night before and she wanted that power transferred to me. She had read in the Bible about how God's healing power was transferred through clothes, and people were healed as a result.*

Tiffany and Gabriel were also in constant prayer. They had put their Dad on a prayer chain with several of their friends in school. They prayed and kept in close contact with me daily.

I did not want anything negative spoken over my husband or to him, nor did I want any negative or hopeless prayers prayed. I remember saying to the Father, "I curse every negative word and prayer spoken over or to my husband in the name of Jesus!" I really did not want anyone going in, feeling sorry for Dean, or thinking that there was no hope. Death and life are in the power of the tongue, and I made sure my tongue spoke life, for THE WORD OF GOD IS LIFE! I did not have time to feel sorry for Dean, and I made no time to feel sorry for him. I felt I was in a battle and I wanted to win."

PROVERBS 18:21 (NKJV)

"Death and life are in the power of the tongue, and they who indulge in it shall eat the fruit of it (for death or life)."

Key 6: *Marilyn protected me from negative people and prayers.*

Key 7: *Marilyn was in this battle to win and whatever sacrifices that took, she was willing to make them.*

Sunday, May 7th—The Word of God was preached to some of us in the waiting area, and we sang praises. We were still not giving up on Dean. My daughter phoned me and told me to read Psalms 40. My son was calling every day to talk to the doctor or nurse about his Dad's condition. There was a time when the thought came to my mind, "get the funeral ready." Immediately, I brought that thought into captivity to the obedience of Christ and I told the devil he was and is a liar. I continued to thank God for His promise in Psalms 103:3, for forgiving all Dean's iniquities, and healing all of Dean's diseases.

PSALM 103:3 (NKJV)

"who forgives all your iniquities, who heals all your diseases"

GLORY! Dean did respond this day but he does not remember. He opened his eyes and looked around as if to say, "What is going on?" I told him I loved him, and so did one of our friends who was with me at the time. The nurse did not want Dean to get too excited, and so increased the sedative which then put him back to sleep.

Key 8: *Marilyn kept her mind on the Word of God, even when it was not looking good for me. She took control of her thinking and kept it on God's promises.*

Monday, May 8th—Dean's parents are here. Praise God! For the next few days my mother-in-law and I sang to Dean, read James 5:13-15, and anointed him with oil. Sometimes Dean's father would go somewhere else to pray.

JAMES 5:13-15 (NKJV)

"Is anyone among you suffering? Let him pray. Is anyone cheerful? Let him sing psalms. Is anyone among you sick? Let him call for the elders of the church, and let them pray over him, anointing him with oil in the name of the Lord. And the prayer of faith will save the sick, and the Lord will raise him up. And if he has committed sins, he will be forgiven."

I was tired in the body, but my spirit was strong. I was so tired one night that when I arrived at the house and turned the car off, I put my head back and fell fast asleep. When I awoke, I went into the house and prayed. I needed His strength to continue. All this had happened so fast and unexpectedly. How could something so minor turn out to be so major, so suddenly? I continued to press in closer to the Lord.

Key 9: *Marilyn kept pressing into God and relying on God's strength.*

During the past days the doctors saw Dean improve and then slip back to where he had been before. One day he would have a temperature. So they would take him to get a CAT scan to see if the infection had spread, and the test would come back negative. His white blood count would go up and the potassium would be low. One day he would be down 50% on the ventilator, and that evening it might go back up. I was still trusting God. Dean was on six different medications. Most of these medications were for his blood pressure. The doctors told me that one of the medicines was detrimental to Dean's health.

One of our friends prayed for Dean with such compassion that he kissed Dean's feet as he was praying for him. He had no idea the condition of my husband's feet. Dean's toes were purple and black from the medicine, and he had lost feeling in them. We found out later that the doctors were planning on cutting his toes off.

Tuesday, May 9th—Dean's healing was taking place quickly. It surprised the doctors and nurses and the other staff who knew of his case. One doctor would say, "He is getting better but we still need to take it slow." Another doctor would say, "Wow, he's improved 200-300% in such a short time."

Many things still happened as Dean's body was healing. The nurse was extremely happy when Dean could follow commands and told the doctor the next day. On the night of May 9th, I came home and purposed in my heart that I would spend all night in prayer for Dean. I found out the next day that a friend had said he was tired of the situation, and so he was in prayer all night also.

Wednesday Morning, May 10th -Five young boys from the high school showed up to pray for Dean during school hours. These boys touched the heart of the male nurse on duty that morning.

He said he would never forget the prayer, love, and the presence he felt in the room while they prayed.

This day he was also taken off the ventilator and dialysis. The nurses asked Dean if he was in any pain, and he shook his head no. They also explained the procedure for removing the breathing tube, and that another breathing treatment would have to be given a half hour later to determine if he could stay off the ventilator.

The nurses told my in-laws and me to take a long lunch break. Prior to leaving for lunch, I spoke in Dean's ear and said to him, "Breathe for me, breathe for your children, and breathe for your friends, BREATHE!" He nodded his head, yes, but he had a puzzled look on his face, as if to say, "What happened?" Dean had this look before but he was unable to speak because of the tube. By this time, Dean was down to taking 1 or 2 medications. Praise God! Psalms 68:35 was one of the scriptures I held on to. I needed God's strength and His power continually.

PSALM 68:35 (NKJV)

> "O God, You are more awesome than your holy places. The God of Israel is He who gives strength and power to His people. Blessed be God!"

Key 10: *Marilyn knew the God whose power and strength were helping her through these long days and nights.*

Upon returning to the hospital after a great lunch with one of our friends, it was awesome to see Dean sitting up in bed. It was good to hear his voice again. It was a great celebration! Many of the nurses who had Dean as a patient came to celebrate his recovery. The nurses were glad to see someone who had made it through. It was also a happy ending to what was Nurse's Week. Other staff came as well to see the progress Dean had made. The only word used to describe Dean was, "Miracle," and boy, did we know that! Some workers who came to visit a couple of days later even called him the "Miracle Man." By now, the fluids were leaving Dean's body and his kidneys were working well.

Then Dean asked the big question, "Would you please sit down and tell me what happened to me?" When I told him, he cried and, of course, I told him more than once. He wanted to know every detail. It really touched him to know that so many people cared and prayed. He was especially touched by those who prayed that we had never met before, and some we have yet to meet. Dean was able to sit up that day for about 15 minutes in a chair. This was the first night I stayed with him. I was his nurse that night.

May 14th, Mother's Day—Dean was moved to another floor. He walked down the long hall to the family visiting room despite not being able to feel his toes. The doctors were still in awe of the miracle that had taken place before their eyes. Dean spent 13 days in the hospital, and 9 of those days were in ICU. "The effective, fervent (red-hot) prayer of a righteous man avails much "(James 5:16). We do give God Almighty all the glory for He is faithful to His Word.

May 16th—Dean came home. He rested and recovered for one and a half months. Then he returned to work, but only for half days for 5 weeks. Dean's toes are now completely healed.

He is not taking any medications. After those 5 weeks, he began working full time. Dean has had several check-ups and tests since he has been home and the doctors have given him a clean bill of health. One doctor told Dean he should tell the story of the miracle that he is still alive. Another doctor told Dean, "A lot of people prayed hard for you." Another said, "I was so scared. I have not been that scared in a long time because things happened so fast."

Dean has been back to the hospital to visit and the staff is still saying what a miracle it was. They even asked him to come one day and make rounds with the doctors, so that others in the hospital could see him. We found out much later that when the doctor blasted the kidney stones, the poisons from the infection got into Dean's bloodstream and caused all of his vital organs to shut down. One nurse told us later that these kinds of cases usually have a bad outcome. Psalm 14:1 says, the fool has said in his heart, "There is no God." Well, there is a God. He is alive, and miracles do happen. He is the Great Jehovah, God Almighty, Lord of Lords and King of Kings! I bless the readers of this testimony in Jesus's name. My prayer for you is that you would take up your cross and follow Jesus daily; that you would live a life pleasing to Him; that He would become the lover of your soul, as He is mine.

In Jesus's name,
Marilyn Braxton

Chapter 5

I Have Seen Jesus

Anthony was a friend of Marilyn and mine. We had met him and his wife four months earlier at a bed and breakfast in a small town in Washington. He and his wife are pastors at a church in Tacoma, Washington. He also worked at Tacoma General Hospital on life support machines. He was assigned that day to help take me off the machine that was helping me breathe. I remember telling him, "I have seen Jesus", and to go tell everyone he knew. As I told him, he just looked at me with a big smile and said, "Yeah, yeah, yeah," with tears coming down his cheeks.

Jesus Is Bright

What did Jesus look like? All I can say is Jesus is bright.* What color is He? I guess I would say bright again, because He was not a real color at all as we know colors here on earth. He was brighter than our sun on a hot sunny afternoon, and yet I was able to look at Him.* It seemed to me that if a being were not RIGHT with Him, that being could be burned up by His brightness and would experience terror.*

Those who were RIGHT with Him could look at Him and would experience perfect joy.* You had to look at Him with a pure heart.* Again, it was more than peace that I felt in Heaven because there just isn't anything that takes away your peace in Heaven.

His Feet

I saw Jesus's feet. They are just like John said in Revelation 1:15.* His feet did look like metal, gold, silver, tin and many more colors of metals, but the light around them really gave off the shine of fine brass. I knew this was the glory of Jesus. He still has the wounds from where the nails pierced His feet.* But what really made an impression upon me was the love His feet showed me. He loved me so much that I did not have to look at His face to experience the love He has for me. I did not have to see another part of Jesus to know how much He loved me. His feet expressed His love for me. If all I saw were His feet, I would still know that He loved me. It was not only that He loved me, but it was like I was the only one He loved in all of His creation.* I knew He loved others but it seemed as if I was the only one. I like to tell others that His feet loved me.

His Hands

Next, I looked at His hands and experienced this same love. Yes, you can see the nail piercings that took place in His hands.* But again, it was the love that was coming out of them to me that expressed His love for me. If I were to have only seen His hands and not another part of Him I would still have known how much He loves me. I sometimes, in telling this part of the story to others, will put my hand in their face telling them that if all you saw was His hand, His hand would say, "I love you and only you." You would know He loves others, but it would still seem as if he only loved you.

Some people have just smiled, others have cried, and still others could only say, "WOW!"

His Body

Just like the Bible says in 1 John 4:7, God is love.* As I looked at the other parts of His body, I experienced over and over again, the love of Jesus just for me, coming from all those different body parts. His body could only express His love for me. I saw what the body of Jesus went through just for me and you. I saw what it cost for me to be there, and to have a relationship with God Almighty. I did not realize before this happened, how great the cost in pain to the physical body of Jesus was, that enabled me and you to have a relationship with God.* He still bears the scars of what He suffered for us. This is best described in the book of Isaiah.

ISAIAH 52:14-15 (NKJV)

> "Just as many were astonished at you, (Jesus) So His visage was marred more than any man, And His form more than the sons of men; So shall He sprinkle many nations. Kings shall shut their mouths at Him; for what had not been told them they shall see, And what they had not heard they shall consider."

Jesus's body showed me why we have the right to have a relationship with God; why we that know Jesus as Lord and Savior, have the right to live forever with God; why we have the right to be in Heaven and not in Hell. Jesus is more beautiful, wonderful, and glorious than I can explain. In Heaven you stop looking at Him with your eyes and start seeing Him from your heart. You get to see Him as He is.* I came to understand that He advocates for us before the Father God with His whole being.*

1 JOHN 2:1 (NKJV)

"My little children, these things I write to you, so that you may not sin. And if anyone sins, we have an Advocate with the Father, Jesus Christ the righteous."

His Face

I was on my hands and knees as I looked into Jesus's face. How do I tell you what His face looks like? His face was as if it were liquid crystal glass made up of pure love, light, and life. I am not saying His face was that, but only that that is what it looked like to me. His face seemed to change as I looked at Him. The shape of His face seemed to change a number of times as I looked at Him. Jesus did have a face like most humans, but instead it would seem to change into different human-like faces.* These were not big changes, but every time I looked at Him, his face seemed to change. I know within me that this change was very important, but at this time I do not have the words to tell what it really means. His face had the colors of the rainbow and colors I cannot describe inside of it.* All these colors appeared at the same time in His face. It has been hard to explain Heaven in English. I know how John and others felt trying to put God into human words.

His face was changing and all the colors were in His face. These colors were changing all the time and they were bright. They were a part of Jesus, and yet, they would leave His being, the colors were alive in themselves. They came out of Him and off of Him as the waves of the ocean flow back and forth on the shore. I was seeing the colors, and yet, I was part of the colors.* I was in the colors, and the colors were coming out of me. I was seeing Jesus, and I was a part of Jesus. I was in Jesus, and Jesus was shining out of me.* I would see the brightness. The brightness was around me. I was part of the brightness, and brightness was shining out of me.* All of it was alive. So what color is Jesus? He is bright. He is not a color as we know colors. Seeing Jesus was glorious! Describing what I saw and felt in human terms does not do justice to what I experienced in Heaven.

When I was looking at the face of Jesus, I did not look at any other part of Him. I just wanted to praise Him. I knew that is what you did when you see Him. I wanted to praise Him forever.

His Head

On Jesus's head was a crown that looked like the sun in all its glory.* This crown was really bright, with rays going up and out into the atmosphere of Heaven.* I could not see any end to the rays. I knew the rays had something to do with healing, but again, I have not found the words or understanding to explain. The rays intertwine with His hair. His hair was like John said in Revelation.*

REVELATION 1:14 (NKJV)

"His head and hair were white like wool, as white as snow"

To me His hair looked more than white and tube-like. The hair-like tubes seemed to wrap around the rays. As I looked at His hair and crown, I again experienced His love for me.

He is Love

Everything about Him is love.* Yes, it is love for you, and it seems as if the love is only for you. You know within that He loves all, but His love for you is so personal that it seems as if it is only for you.* You know He has cared for you since the beginning and will continue to care for you forever.* You do not want to leave this kind of outpouring of love for you. His love is alive. It is more than just an emotion.

His brightness is before you, around you, part of you and in you. And one more thing, you are becoming His love. Yes, you are His love. Jesus truly loves us.

Chapter 6

My God Is

Before you read my daughter's account of what she experienced when I died, here is a little background on Tiffany A. Wright (Braxton). She was attending Northwestern University which is near Chicago, Illinois. She was in her third year there when this happened to me in 2006. She graduated with a degree in teaching in 2007. She has been walking with Jesus for a number of years now, and has led many people to Jesus while attending college. Our Father God has blessed her in a number of ways over the years and this is just one. As you read, you can see that her first love is God. Read and enjoy her story while growing in the knowledge of our Lord Jesus.

Tiffany's Testimony

I have to say that my experience with the death and later recovery of my dad was during a very significant time in my relationship with God. I admit that there were times when I thought that I might lose my father during those early days in the hospital. I thought of how he might never see me get married, and that my future children would grow up without his spiritual guidance as an amazing grandfather.

This was a huge testing time for me!

When I found out that my dad was in the hospital, I initially did not think much of it. He was having kidney stone problems and had had this problem before. Even when I found out he was going into surgery, I was not alarmed because I had actually been with him when the doctors had removed kidney stones years before. I was not really concerned until I got the call from my mother, "Tiffany, they had to do CPR on your father! Pray!"

I got this call at a very convenient "God moment." I was going to the International House of Prayer in Chicago weekly on Friday nights. The previous week, a man came and spoke about whether we truly believe that God is the Living God. I went through the week saying to myself "God, you are the Living God." As I meditated on this truth, it became very real to me, and so I decided that I would not allow any further issues of doubt about whether God is living, good and/ or faithful within my being. I got Mom's call after I made this decision.

I called my boyfriend, Jason, who is now my husband immediately. He said he would be praying and assured me not of God's goodness, but of the faithfulness of God. Thankfully, my good friend, Jen, was also there with me for support. She has always been that person for me that I know I can trust, no matter what the situation. So I told her about Dad, and she had nothing but smiles for me as she prayed with me for my father. She told me that she felt God was telling her that it was all going to work out well.

I prayed the rest of the way home, and all that night I was in and out of sleep. When I woke up, I knew I had to get out of my dorm, so I could really pray. Thankfully, my friend Cory, who had also been with us the previous night, was going to the House of Prayer during the day. I gladly went with him.

When I got to the House of Prayer, I sat for a while, rejecting the doubt and questions that my mind was being flooded with. Jason called me and told me he had been out in the woods praying for my family and my dad all day. He once again made sure that I did not doubt that my father would live. Jason was so important in making sure that I dealt with any doubts that came up and that I did not even play with them in my head.

When I called Mom that day, I had the opportunity to pray for my father over the phone. My mom put the phone up to his ear and I prayed over him. This was one of the most difficult moments in my life, and at a time when I was glad that I was not there with him. In between the tears, I was able to pray a prayer of faith over him.

When I went back into the House of Prayer, I prayed for Dad's healing even more so, and was reminded of the passage when David loses his son. David fasts and prays for his baby boy until the baby dies. Immediately after he dies, David goes to the temple to worship the Lord. In remembering this passage of the Bible, I thought about David's reliance on God no matter what the situation was, and how David still recognized God's goodness no matter what. I really checked my heart for any wrongs I might have within.

These were two main things that I felt I had to deal with before I prayed because I wanted to pray with a pure heart and an undivided heart. I did not believe my dad would die, but I needed to make sure that I was not praying out of selfishness, but I truly wanted God's will to be done. First, I made certain that no matter what happened, I would continue to pray for the sick even if my dad died. This was because I needed to have a pure heart that served God alone and not outcomes. Secondly, I searched within myself to make sure that I would not blame God if Dad did die. I would not think of God as being bad or unfaithful to me or His promises, no matter what happened.

So, I then began to pray, most of it being simple worship for the Living God. I wrote the following about God as I focused on His goodness:

> *"My God is faithful, My God is holy, My God is wonderful,*
> *My God is mighty, My God is magnificent, My God is glorious,*
> *My God is powerful, My God is victorious, My God is God,*
> *My God reigns, My God is love"*
>
> Tiffany A. Wright

On March 29, 2008, I walked my daughter down the aisle to marry Jason Gomillion Wright. I could not have picked a better man to marry my daughter. It was a great day for me to see my daughter, Tiffany, get married. I am even more looking forward to being a grandfather to their wonderful children!

Chapter 7

What Did I See in Heaven?

When I died, I knew where to go. There was no one telling me where to go.* I was almost like a salmon going home. No one had to tell me. When I got there, I knew I was supposed to be there. I was in my place. Everything was RIGHT. I was right where I was supposed to be. I was home. I was home. I WAS HOME!

What is that home like? It is not like our homes here on earth. First, everything in Heaven is alive. Everything is alive and there is nothing dead there.* I understood then that true death was not having the Father God or Jesus or the Holy Spirit in your life.* True death is not having God as your Lord and Savior.

Back From the Dead?—On the Contrary

I thought that when you died here on earth that was the death the Bible talks about. But, when you are in Heaven, you know that death is not being in relationship with God. When I first arrived in Heaven, I knew that because of what Jesus did, I was with the Father and Jesus, and I knew I was truly alive. Everyone on earth always says I came back from the dead. On the other hand, even some for fun would say, I was a dead man walking. No! I was alive with the Father and Son.*.

MATTHEW 22:32 (NKJV)

"I am the God of Abraham, the God of Isaac, and the God of Jacob."

God is not the God of the dead, but of the living. God has not stopped creating life. I thought it was finished when man and woman were created, but that is not so. Everything is alive where Jesus and the Father are. He does not live in or with death. Our God is pure life, light, and love.* You become what He is: life, light, and love. Life is everywhere in Heaven and life is everything in Heaven. Life is Heaven itself. We here on earth live with death, and think there is an end to everything, but in Heaven life goes on and on.

As I said earlier, everything in Heaven is alive. The light-like buildings which looked like light but were not light, the landscape, and the atmosphere were all alive.* The buildings look almost like glass, but they are alive and not glass. They shine with the glory of the Lord. They also can move around from place to place. The buildings are in cities across Heaven. What we would call "landscape" was alive. The trees, flowers, bushes, grass, mountains, hills, valleys, lakes, rivers, and much more that I do not have words for were all living.

Heaven is Huge

Because of coming from earth and living with death, a thought went through my thinking, "Aren't we going to run out of room in Heaven?" After all, there is no death and everything keeps on living.* This thought was in and out of my thoughts. It did not have to be answered because it needed not to be asked. There is more room in Heaven than we think. There is room for all God has created and will create.

Heaven is big, large, huge, extensive, spacious, and expanding.* Our universe is like a fragment of protons or neutrons compared to Heaven. In other words, this universe is very, very, very small compared to Heaven.

I came to understand that Heaven is always expanding, becoming larger even as you read this book. There seemed to be no end to Heaven. After a moment the size of Heaven became unimportant. I was with Jesus. That was all that counted. All I can tell people is that where God is, IS BIG! *

Distance and Time

Even though there is more space in Heaven than here on earth, there is no distance in Heaven, as we know it here on earth. I seemed to be far from things and yet near. I seemed to be close to the Father's throne and yet far away. If I wanted to be somewhere else in Heaven I just had to think it and I was there.* For instance, if I had that ability here on earth and wanted to be around the world in China from Seattle, Washington, in the United States, all I would have to do is think China, and I would be there. Then again, I could be back in Seattle by just thinking Seattle, Washington.

How long did I stay there? The hospital transcripts say that I had what they call a Prolonged Cardiac Arrest for 1 hour and 45 minutes. The doctor said I was "really, really dead" .To me it seemed as if I was in Heaven a long time and yet a very short time. I had experienced eternity. Even now, life here seems very short. I know I will outlast every problem that comes my way and someday soon, I will be with Jesus.* I hope you, that are reading this now, can come to that understanding. If you know Jesus as your Lord and Savior, you will outlive every problem you are facing right now and every problem you will ever face on this earth. That is Good News!

I came to understand that whether it is 50 years or 500 years, it will be short compared to eternity. How do you put time on eternity? Why would you put time on eternity?* Why do we put time on earth? We use time on earth because we are counting down to the end of time here on earth. There is no end of time in Heaven. Jesus said He is the beginning and end.

REVELATION 1:8 (NKJV)

"I am the Alpha and the Omega, the Beginning and the End, says the Lord, who is and who was and who is to come, the Almighty."

The Father said He is "I AM" in Exodus.

EXODUS 3:14 (NKJV)

"And God said to Moses, "I AM WHO I AM." "

The Holy Spirit is everywhere all at the same time: past, present, and future, as Genesis 1:1-2 and John 14:16 states.

GENESIS 1:1-2 (NKJV)

"In the beginning God created the heavens and the earth. The earth was without form, and void; and darkness was on the face of the deep. And the Spirit of God was hovering over the face of the waters."

John 14:16 (NKJV)

"And I will pray the Father, and He will give you another Helper (Holy Spirit), that He may abide with you forever."

So how and why would we have a measurement of time in Heaven? It really is everlasting eternity. Because there is no time in Heaven, there is no age or aging there. Everything is new every moment. That is hard for us to grasp here on earth, but the fact is, there is just no time in Heaven. You are outside of time there. Everything is now.

The Atmosphere in Heaven

Heaven has the most beautiful atmosphere that has ever been created. I hear people talking about the atmosphere here on earth, and how great the sunrise or sunset looks. The most wonderful or gorgeous sky you can ever see here on earth cannot even come close to the atmosphere in Heaven. I start out by saying it is bright because of the glory of our God. Jesus and the Father light up everything. There is no darkness in Heaven. *

I remember looking out of the car window when my wife was driving me home from the hospital. That day was a bright, sunny May day here in the beautiful Northwest. Since it rains a lot in Washington State, a clear day seems especially beautiful. The vegetation is green, the sky and water are so blue, and you can see Mount Rainier which is over 14,000 feet high to the east and the Cascade Mountain range. To the west, you can see the Olympic Mountains. This was one of those days in the Seattle area, and I was looking out the car window with a frown on my face. My wife looked at me and asked me what was wrong. All I could say was, "It is so dull here." In my heart, I was thinking how dull this whole world is compared to Heaven. I sometimes try very hard to make this place seem beautiful in my mind. I know it is for many people, but because I have experienced the atmosphere of Heaven, I just do not feel that same way any longer.

Jesus and the Father light up everything in Heaven. Their glory and light shine out of everything. Darkness cannot hide anywhere in Heaven. The atmosphere in Heaven is something you can experience and not just see. It is a golden, a yellow, and a white. An artist that I know says it sounds like sunrise colors.* The atmosphere in Heaven reminded me of the rising of the sun on a clear morning here on earth. The atmosphere had the rainbow colors and even more colors moving throughout it. The atmosphere looked like curtains moving on a windy day. It looked like a waterfall in reverse. It would be as if you were looking at one of the great waterfalls on this earth and see the water going up the fall and not down. The curtains looked like the Aurora Borealis Lights, also known as the Northern Polar Lights in the north polar zone, or the Aurora Australis, also known as the Southern Lights in the south polar zone. But again, the atmosphere was a golden yellow that was alive. I first came to really see how alive it was when it bowed when Jesus said to me the last time, "No, It is not your time. Go back." The atmosphere just folded over and bowed.

The Colors in Heaven

Colors in Heaven are bright. I used to say that the dullest color there is brighter than the brightest color here. But, there are no dull colors in Heaven. There are colors there we cannot see here on earth, and there are more colors in Heaven than you can even imagine. Jesus and the Father give off living colors, and they are beautiful, so beautiful. Everything has a color or colors to it. When I saw Jesus, He is bright and the Father is bright, along with beings that shine. The best way to describe the colors I saw there is to compare them to the colors of the rainbow. But even that does not really do justice to the colors alive in Heaven. There are more colors in Heaven than on any rainbow we see here on earth, and many more colors than I could even imagine.

The colors of flowers here on earth are the closest to the colors I experienced in Heaven and yet, even the colors of these flowers have lost their glory compared to the colors in Heaven.* Colors in Heaven are original colors. They are like our primary colors here on earth. God does not mix one color with another to make new color there. Each color is an original color. The red is red, the purple is purple, the green is green, and so on and so on. Every color there is its own color. There are no shades of a color. Expect to see colors that will put you in awe when you get to Heaven. The colors on earth do not come close to what you experience in Heaven. The colors are alive, along with everything else.

Jesus' Words Are Alive

I have said earlier that Jesus spoke to me with His voice. His voice is love. His voice is mighty. His voice left Him with power and authority, but when it got to me, it was life and comfort.* Yes, life for me! It was alive when it entered into me, and as I said before, I knew that I had to go back to the earth. The rest of the moments He spoke to me were just from His heart, just like everything else there.

Communication in Heaven

Here on earth words that are spoken are very important to us. Without the spoken word, communication between people here on earth can be very difficult. But, I felt that speaking words in Heaven was a waste of energy or just not important.* Jesus and the Father thought something and it was transferred to me. The other beings formed a thought, and it was transferred to me.* There seemed to be no need to express that thought aloud again. In Heaven you lack nothing. You do not have any shortcomings. You are perfect, as your Creator is perfect. That is the way it is with all of God's creation there. Because everything is alive they can all communicate with you.* All of life there formed thoughts, and those thoughts were transferred to me. It was a faster and clearer form of communication with everything in Heaven.

Everything was RIGHT, so there was no miscommunication with each other.* There were no misunderstandings with each other. There was nothing you would have to hide from each other. We all had pure thoughts and every thought was pure.* There was a rule that you did not go into any of the Heavenly creations' thoughts without first receiving permission. Satan, the last being that broke the rule, is no longer there in Heaven. Imagine the power we would have if we really understood the power of our thoughts. *

Everyone and Everything Praised the Lord

The only time I saw beings open their mouths was when they were singing praises to the Father at the throne. Every living being and creature praises the Father and Jesus. Every part of God's creation praises God all the time, and no one else receives praise, only God.* When you are in Heaven you know that is what you do.* It is similar to breathing air here on earth. A baby does not need to be taught how to breathe. He or she knows what to do as soon as he or she is born. I too knew what to do, and I seemed to live off the praise. You were alive in Heaven because of God himself and nothing else.

To hear the flowers praise the Lord is wonderful. The birds sing praise to the Lord. Water praised the Lord. Mountains praised the Lord. Praise came from the atmosphere. Praise was in the atmosphere. Praise was the atmosphere. We all praised Him repeatedly, over and over again.* You never seemed to run out of things to praise Him for. I can remember thanking Him over and over for being there and loving me so much. I thanked Him for loving everyone here on earth. I thanked Him for making me. I thanked Him over and over. I know I could have gone on forever with my praises.

Writing this down reminds me of the fact, that praise did not ever leave my thinking when I was in Heaven.* I still praise Him all the time here on earth. It is sometimes hard for me to stop and to think about other things. It is hard for other people to understand this because in praising of Him I am focused on the MOST important FOREVER thing to me, and what others may see or think is important here on earth is temporal and so fades away into unimportance to me. Those of you that know Jesus as your Lord and Savior will share this same experience.

When I first left the hospital and was at home, I would wake up early to see the day "awake". That is what I called it. Really, I just wanted to hear the birds sing and see the sun come up. The birds in Heaven always praised the Lord with their songs. The birds here on earth do the same, most of the time. When the sun comes up, it seems to me to be saying, "Praise the Lord." So, I wanted to see this "awakening" take place every morning, and take part with these creations of God in saying, "Praise the Lord." Every living being and creature praises the Father and Jesus.

Our Connection in Heaven

One of the most fascinating things I experienced in Heaven was being connected to everything there at the same moment. Because of this, I came to understand life in heaven very quickly. It is almost like the electricity that connects power to run anything that needs electric energy here. It is similar to our computer system that is connected to the Internet and in turn connects us to every computer in the world. God is the connection between each and every one of His creations.* This gave me great understanding of what I say.

Relating My Experience to You

There is no substance on earth that can come close to the substance God used to create everything in Heaven. There is no sin to corrupt what God has made.* His creations in Heaven are in their purest form. There is no sin to destroy what God has made. Therefore all I can tell you, and describe, is what something is like in Heaven. If you have what some call, "an out of body experience", afterwards you can only relate what you saw from an earthly point of view because, after the experience, you have lost the God connection to everything. I have come to believe that only those who have truly died can tell you what they saw from a heavenly point of view. The reason is because their body which stayed here on earth became disconnected from the real them, their spirit.

When I was there, I did not want to come back, and I was planning on staying. So, I understand what John who wrote Revelations,

Ezekiel, Daniel and David who wrote most of the Psalms went through in trying to tell others about Heaven in earthly terms. As you read on, and if you read the writings of these men in the Bible, you will see that each uses the word "like" a lot, to try to tell us what they saw. I have already used a lot of examples in this book to help you see what I saw or hear what I heard. But understand, as much as I try to convey my thoughts to others, I am still coming up way short of what it is really like in Heaven. This God connection to everything in Heaven helped me to understand what was going on there, but I feel my explanation here on earth is lacking the correct words.

One of the best ways I have found for people to connect with what I experienced in Heaven is through the Bible. I have found approximately 90% of what I explain about Heaven somewhere in the Bible. I have met with my Pastor and Assistant Pastor for almost two years now, reviewing what I experienced in Heaven. We have worked together to find verses in the Bible that relate to a specific event that I experienced in Heaven. I knew from what Jesus downloaded inside of me that I would find everything I saw in Heaven in the Bible. He is not hiding Heaven from us. We have just limited our thinking to what we have and know here on earth.

Some have said that God did not put everything in the Bible, and I say that, that is most likely true. But I say to those that say that, until you can tell me everything in the Bible you cannot stand on that statement. I have found so much in the Bible of what I experienced in Heaven. Finding the right earthly words is the hard part.

Chapter 8

God of Miracles

My son, Gabriel A. Braxton, was 19 years old and was attending Christ for the Nations Bible College in Dallas, Texas. He had a host of friends around his age that loved the Lord Jesus. Many of these young men and women, he led to the Lord. A number of his friends prayed and helped him through this trying time. A few of them even came to the hospital to pray for me when Gabriel was still in Texas. His account of the story is taken out of his journal. As you read on you will feel the love that my son had for me as he was faced with his father's death.

Gabriel's Testimony

May 11th, 2006—This last week has been crazy! I did not journal for the past seven days because of some events that happened. What I did not mention, is what happened on May 4th that had to do with my dad. He went into the hospital (St. Francis) because of a kidney stone. I did not think of it as a big deal, but my mom called, and asked for me to pray, and so, I did. I found out my dad had kidney stones and an infection and the doctors were pumping him with antibiotics to get the infection out of his system. It was a miracle that he was able to drive and to walk into the hospital by himself. Kidney stones can cause serious pain.

The next day, May 5th, I found out that my dad had to have surgery to remove the stones. I was calling my mom a lot because I wanted to know about Dad. Throughout that day, I had been praying for my dad and some of my friends had been praying for him as well. My friends, Tomo, Luke, and Joe, and I went to the Rangers game. It was pretty fun until I got a call from my mom. It was an urgent serious call. She told me that the doctors were doing CPR on my dad. His heart had stopped. That changed the course of the night.

Tomo, Luke, Joe, and I prayed, and afterwards I walked out to the food area. There I began to pray again. This time I would prophesy over my dad, saying that he would live and not die. I bound the devil and commanded my dad's body to work properly. It was intense! I tried to call people and ask them to pray, but at first, I could not get in touch with anyone.

Staring at Six Flags from the balcony of the stadium in Dallas, Texas, I started to hate the fact that I was so many miles away from my dad. Joe walked out. I forget what he said, but we left. I did not stop praying. I kept praying because I was determined. I knew it was God's will to heal my dad. On the ride back in the car, I called my mom, but Francine, a friend, answered the phone. After an hour and a half, my dad was finally stable. What a relief! Well, a little relief. Joe thanked God for answering his prayer by performing a miracle.

I had lost my huge appetite, and I just wanted to go home and pray. We got back to the G, the guys' tower at the college, and I went upstairs. I met Sam, and he and I went to his room and prayed. Later he told me he really did not think it would make sense for my dad to die. In fact, during the prayer time, Sam said to God, "It does not make sense to me why Gabe and his sister would have to grow up without a father." After a while, he went out with his girlfriend at the time, but said that I could stay in the room and pray. Of course, I did. I prayed, prophesied, commanded, and pleaded. I put all that I had learned about healing into practice, and I refused to back down. Curfew was 1 o'clock that night so I planned to pray until at least 12:30 AM.

During my prayer time, I called my mom to see how my dad was doing. She said that he was urinating which was good because that meant that his kidneys were functioning properly. Around 12:15 AM, I went to Joe, Luke, and Michael's room to see if Luke would take me somewhere to get something to eat. I did not have much of an appetite but I knew I should have something to eat. They were all asleep, so Luke did not really want to get up and drive me somewhere at the time. I called Joe's girlfriend, Abbie who is now his wife, and I asked if she would take me somewhere. She said she would. Her roommate, Rhea, prayed with her father about my dad. Rhema said both she and her dad felt a strong anointing. Her father had a huge burden for my dad, and the next day they would have the Church pray for him. What a blessing!

While I was waiting downstairs in the bottom of the G, Luke called me and asked where I was. He changed his mind about taking me, but Abbie and Rhema were already on their way. Luke decided to go with us too. Joe really had God's favor shine upon him. Abbie is an amazing person. She is so loving and caring. It's amazing. She takes care of Luke and me, too. It's really sweet of her. She drove us to Sonic and I ordered a chili dog. The drive and talk with my friends really encouraged me. We had a few laughs and that was good.

When I got back, I called my mom to see how she was doing. She was crying and saying that she missed my dad. She wanted him to come home. I tried to encourage her, but it was sad and after that, I could not eat. I had a few bites of the chili dog and put it in the fridge. I finally, drifted off to sleep.

The next day, May 6th, I decided I would spend the day in the prayer room. I was just going to grab my phone charger, my laptop, my pillow, and camp out, but before I went to the prayer room, my mom called. She told me that they wanted to transfer my dad to Tacoma

General Hospital to have him undergo dialysis because his kidneys were not functioning too well anymore. It was our choice to decide. This was hard because we have had some bad experiences with hospitals in the past. She told me to call my sister, Tiffany, and ask her what she thought.

After I got off the phone, I began to cry. I did not know what to do. I told God, I am only 19. I told Him that I didn't know anything about medical stuff. I didn't even want to have a say in it. Then, I called Tiffany. My sister told me to tell my mom to pray about it and decide. I called my mom back, and she had the nurse explain some about what dialysis was and how it worked to me. Personally, I was going to say no, but after I talked with the nurse, it was easier for me to trust the hospital and the doctor. My mom gave the ok for the transfer.

I cannot recall everything that happened during this time. I do a horrible job of mentioning all the people that found time to pray for my dad with me. It was something extremely awesome to see and experience. Everyone kept speaking blessings over my dad saying that he would live and that he was going to be all right. I called my mom a lot to see how my dad was doing.

Later that day, I told my friend, Andrew, what was going on, and he prayed. Then, he spoke a word over me that I knew was true. He told me to stay strong in faith. I think he even gave me a scripture, but I don't remember. He also told me not to waiver in unbelief and he said, "I do not believe you are doing that." I knew that I wasn't wavering. I knew that the grace of Jesus empowered me to not lose faith, to not lose heart, and to continue in intercession. I called out prophesies that had been spoken over my dad's life and I said they would continue. My dad always said our family was a team, so I called my mom and sister and prayed with them, claiming that the leader of this team would not be taken away. I started to think about the situation. Then I received a revelation. The devil wanted to take out my dad's kidneys because the kidneys dispose of the toxins in the body and this connected spiritually with my dad. My dad had a huge burden to rid sin out of his life, like the kidneys do for the body, so the devil was attacking the physical to destroy the spiritual.

Also, the devil wanted Dad's heart because my dad has a huge heart for people. He loves so much and Satan hates that. So I sent a text message to those who were praying for him and told them what Satan was trying to do. I told them to claim that he would continue to get the sin out of his life, and his heart would continue to grow in love for people. Then, I called my mom and sister and told them. After an intense day of prayer, I was encouraged.

Luke and I went to get a smoothie, and then we gathered in his room with Mike and David. I have to admit, we talked about girls and Luke's latest crush. It was good fellowship. I heard that my dad was doing better and I fell asleep in the room. I woke up at 12:59 AM and ran back to room 406 because curfew was at 1:00 AM.

On Sunday morning, May 7th, I got a call from Joe. We decided to go to Mary Martha's, the girls' dorm, for dinner. We had ribs, and spent a quiet day together as friends.

Monday, May 8th—I had an exam for my class on the Life and Teachings of Christ. I didn't really study for it because of all the things that were taking place. I think I did well though. During these days I prayed for my dad a lot and called the hospital a lot to see how he was doing. People prayed with me. When I would call, the nurse gave some good reports, and some were not so good. Even though the report was not always good, I still chose to believe God's report. I chose to believe my dad was healed by the stripes of Jesus.

That day I went out to eat at Chipotle's with Luke and Joe. It was fun. I learned what to get and how to eat the burrito they made for me. I started out using utensils but that was not really working. I should have looked at the directions on the napkin.

I am not so sure what I did on Tuesday, May 9th, but that night I went to Bennigans' with some friends. While we were there, I learned that my dad was having a rough time in the hospital. My mom told me that my dad was crying some that day. That was one of the things I didn't want to hear. After I heard that, I was so sad. I had to pray.

I stepped outside and began to pray. While I was outside, I called the nurse and she told me that my dad was on 100% oxygen. That was not good because he had just been on 50%. My friends and I made it home about 20 minutes before curfew. I asked Wade, one of the Room Assistants (RA) on our floor, if I could go to the prayer room. He said yes, and Sam who was another RA, suggested that I go to the eighth floor prayer room. If it was locked, I should go to the prayer room on the first floor. So I went up to room 807 and Andrew was in there. He joined me in praying for my dad for about 25 minutes.

The next morning, May 10th, I woke up at 5:00 AM to pray for my dad. I couldn't stop praying. That day I had decided to read Proverbs 10. It was the chapter for my dad. I wanted him off the ventilator and that chapter has many promises concerning your mouth. I claimed the blessings of the chapter in my dad's life. I couldn't stop praying that morning. I prayed for him all the way through chapel, which ended at 8:40 AM. That day, we had an exam for Fred's Evangelism class. I think I did fairly well, though again I did not study that much.

Wednesday was a big day. It was my last day of college before summer break. After school that day, Luke, Michael, Joe, and I went out to T.G.I. Friday's to eat. While we were there, I saw a kid in a wheel chair that I wanted to pray for. He was sitting at a table with other young kids and some adults who were taking care of them. I went up to one of the adult ladies and asked if I could pray for the kid in the wheelchair. She said she didn't mind but insisted that I pray for all of them as well. So I prayed for them all. That was such a blessing.

During that day my mom called me and told me some extraordinary news. She told me of the miracle that had occurred that day that had shocked the doctors and had the whole floor of the hospital rejoicing. The doctors had taken the ventilator out of my dad's mouth, and he was doing well! He was even speaking, which was really cool to hear.

One of the best things that Mom shared was some news that Dad gave my mom. He told her that he had died three times, each time seeing Jesus, and Jesus telling him to go back because it was not his time. My dad came out of his sedation with many words to tell people and a lot of information that Jesus had shared with him. How exciting! I told some people and rejoiced myself. After running around helping Joe find some things that he needed, we finally settled down to have my last night with them at Applebee's. Joe, Abbie, Luke, and I had a good time, rejoicing in the good news about my dad.

That night, I slept in Joe, Luke, and Michael's room because earlier that day I had checked out of my room. Later that night, Hannah, the daughter of Ron Luce from Teen Mania called. I had the chance to tell her about the awesome testimony of my dad. She said it encouraged her as she had been having a rough day. That night I went to sleep on the reclining chair in their room. It was really comfortable but I still had a bit of a rough night.

My alarm went off at 5:00 AM. It was May 11th and my flight back home to Seattle, Washington, was going to start boarding at 6:30 AM. Luke and Joe woke up and helped me take my stuff downstairs. I look back on that morning and it's sad, because I knew I would miss those guys. My Uncle Larry arrived at 5:30 AM, and Luke, Joe, and I said our good-byes.

I arrived at the airport around 6:00 AM. I had two big suitcases, and one of them was super heavy. When I got to the baggage check-in line, the first bag went in okay. I figured I would have to pay extra for the really heavy one. I put it on the scale and it weighed about 70 something pounds. The guy told me I'd have to pay $25. That was okay with me because I expected that. He was doing a few things, and then all of a sudden, he told me I could go. So, I didn't have to pay.

Jesus reveals Himself to me through things like these. Such a blessing!

The plane ride went well. I sat next to a guy named Ron and he was really nice. Ron and his wife are Southern Baptist and they were on their way to Seattle to catch a cruise to Alaska. When our food came, I asked Ron if he wanted to pray with me. I was sitting in the end seat C and he was sitting in the middle seat B with his wife to the left of him in seat A. I leaned over and prayed aloud for the food. The rest of the flight went well. Towards the end of the flight, Ron handed me a card and told me he wanted to take me out to eat next time I am in Texas. That was nice of him.

When I arrived in Seattle, Washington, my Uncle Lewis picked me up from the airport. We drove to my house and dropped my stuff off. My mom was there and it was good to see her. Then, we went to pick up my grandma and grandpa, and once we got them, we headed to the hospital. I saw my dad and I got to hug him. It was exciting. Of course, I did not like seeing him in the hospital, but I was just glad to see him. I did not like being so far away when all those frightening things were happening to him. He lifted up three fingers and told me he saw Jesus three times. He started to cry when he said this.

After I visited with my dad, my mom took me home so I could shower and then rest. I went back later and stayed the night with my dad. When it was time to sleep though, the nurses and doctors told us that they were going to be waking us up periodically throughout the night. My dad told me to hold his hand as we fell asleep listening to Psalms.

On Friday, May 12th, my dad had to get another PICC-line, like an IV line, put in the thick vein right above his heart. I didn't like having to give my input on decisions like this. The doctor went over a list of all the things that could go wrong. My grandma, grandpa, mom, dad, and I prayed about what to do. If we did not have the PICC-line put in, the veins in my dad's left arm would have been destroyed because the IV medication they recently had put in him was not meant to go through small veins. After some prayer, I brought the list over to my mom and said, "I figured it out. "You see these?" I pointed to the bad side effects. I said, "These are all just fears and God did not give us a spirit of fear." So, God's word gave me comfort about the situation. My grandpa then said we should do it. My grandma agreed, and I too said we should do it. My mom said to go through with it, and my dad said he felt secure about it.

After the decision was set, I was still a little anxious. I did not want my dad to talk, and I did not want to be in the room. I just wanted them to put the PICC-line in and take that other IV out of his arm. I decided to go home rather than watch and wait for them to put in the PICC-line.

I prayed the whole way home and called Joe to pray as well. When I got home, I spent the next hour praying for my dad. I know many people do not believe in perfection, but I wanted what the doctors were doing to be perfect. My dad had told me to call Pastor Steve and let him know that he was in the hospital and to send him a personal message about friendship as well. I called him and we prayed for my dad.

After about an hour, I called my mom to see what was going on. Inserting the PICC-line was successful. Later that night, I went back to the hospital since Mom was doing the day shifts with Dad and I was doing the night shift. I put my chair up to the bed and fell asleep next to my dad. I had a good night's rest that night. We had Christian music playing in the background. It was great. Throughout these days, I would help him eat and get him things. It was good for my mom and me to have been there. After a night with my dad, I left Saturday morning.

It was May 13th. When I got home, I called Lennie and asked him if he would like to come over. I asked him to mow the lawn as well, and he was nice enough to do so. Lennie and I rode around before we went to visit my dad, and while we were there, Pastor Steve and Beth dropped in for a visit as well. They brought my dad a shirt that Josh, Pastor Steve's son, had designed for an event he founded called Repossess.

While Pastor Steve and Beth visited with my dad, Lennie and I left. We went to Arby's and met up with Luke. From there, we went to the Christian bookstore to try to find my mom a Mother's Day gift. I didn't know what to get her. Lennie had a brilliant plan. He told me to get my mom some Ranger Cookies from Marlene's. Perfect! She had not had them in a long time and she would always ask me to get some for her. So, I got a card and headed over to Marlene's. As Lennie and I walked up, Marlene's was closing, but the lady let us in to grab the cookies. That was so nice of her. Afterwards, we all went to eat at Chipotle's. Then, I went back to the hospital. That night was rough for me. I was sick, and I felt horrible, so I left at 3:00 AM.

It was Mother's Day, May 14, and I woke up after a rough night. I went to my parents' room and worked some on the computer. After a while, I left to go be with my dad. Earlier that day I had found out that they were moving my dad out of ICU. That was good. So, when I got there, my dad was in a regular hospital room. They brought me a cot to sleep on for the night. That night I served my dad and helped him out a lot. It was rough. We were up just about every hour, with nurses coming in and out of the room, and my dad having nightmares. So we prayed and turned on some Christian music. I think that helped a bit. Around 6:00 AM, my dad woke me up and told me to leave, so I could go home and get some rest. I thought it was funny. Here we are awake almost all night, and finally, when I do fall asleep, he tells me to leave. Ha-ha! That's okay though. That's my dad, in the hospital, and yet, putting others before himself. I went home and slept.

May 15th, I woke up around 3:00 PM, and immediately I had to get up. I didn't do much today. I printed out resumes to get a job this summer, and then around 6, I started to pray for about 45 minutes. My sister was flying in today. Her flight was going to land at 7:45 PM, and I was going to be the one to pick her up. After praying, I headed to the airport to get my sister. It was good to see her. We headed off to the hospital after that.

When we got to the hospital, my dad was happy to see my sister, but since he had other visitors inside the room, we waited outside in the waiting room with our grandma and grandpa. The other visitors left and my sister and I had the chance to see our dad. I was coughing a lot so my dad said I could not stay. He wanted me to go home and rest. He said he would be okay. I wanted to stay but I think he said what was best.

May 16, 2006—Today was a cool day. My dad came home. That was exciting...and Jesus is amazing!"

—Gabriel Braxton

Chapter 9

The True Gatekeeper of Heaven

I came to understand who the real gatekeeper of Heaven is. It is Jesus and only Jesus.* I understood this the last time He told me to "Go Back." I saw in His eyes the love for humanity. I saw the love for every girl, boy, woman and man.

I Looked Into Jesus's Eyes

The eyes of Jesus are like flames of fire with changing colors of red, orange, blue, green, yellow, and many other colors within them. John said in Revelation 1:14, that "His eyes (are) like a flame of fire".*

Jesus's eyes are deep wells full of life. I felt that I could get lost in His eyes when I looked into them, and I would never want to come out. Again, at first it seemed as if His eyes only had love for me, but, when I thought about someone else, I saw the love He had for them within His eyes. It was like He loved only them. So I thought about someone else and the same thing happened. I saw Jesus's love for them. I did this with a number of heavenly beings and a few people here on earth. In His eyes I saw the love for every human and creation of God.

I saw in the eyes of Jesus that He wanted everyone in Heaven who is still alive on this earth.* He did not want to lose one person to Hell. Jesus wants all people saved and living eternally with Him in Heaven. I wish we could understand just how much the Father, Jesus, and Holy Spirit love each of us. When I looked into Jesus's eyes, I saw this love, and I knew I became that love also. If we have Jesus, we all have that love within us and should be becoming His love for others.

He Loves Us No Matter What

While I was looking into Jesus's eyes, we had this communication in our thoughts. No words were spoken, but I said to Him, "Even child molesters?" I had worked with children and teenagers over the past 33 years. During that time, the one issue that came up frequently with those children was sexual abuse by adults. This one issue, to me, seemed to do more damage to those children than all the other issues I faced as a counselor. I have seen many people who recovered from many types of abuse, but every time I had to deal with someone who had been sexually abused, the damage seemed to be the most harmful and recovery would be the most difficult. I would always get upset and frustrated with these kinds of cases.

Jesus said back to me, "When a person is placed in jail, they get out. They either get out when their sentence has been served, or they get out when they die, but they get out. But when a person goes to Hell, he or she is there for eternity." Then His eyes looked at me with the fiery red flame and said, "WHO ARE YOU TO NULLIFY WHAT I HAVE DONE?"* This came across to me in a very stern manner. I saw Jesus's arms outstretched like He was on the cross and I knew He had paid the price THEN for everyone who had sinned or would ever sin. We do not have a right to condemn anyone, since He does not. I knew that I knew! He wanted all people there with Him. Sin is sin. There are no exceptions to what He did on the cross. All the Father asks for is our acceptance and love for His son Jesus. He truly wants all people there with Him in Heaven. All people!

Aunt Barbara

I remember seeing one of my relatives in Heaven that on earth, I never believed would have made it to Heaven. That was my Aunt Barbara. My Aunt Barbara was my favorite aunt. She lived close to us when I was growing up in California. She would come and take care of us when our parents would go out of town. She was fun to be around, and I could not wait to see her when she came around.

However, the side that I saw of Aunt Barbara when she was on earth did not lead me to believe that she was a Christian on her way to Heaven. But when I was in Heaven, guess who was there? Yes, Aunt Barbara! She must have accepted Jesus as Lord and Savior. That is the only way to get into Heaven. Since I did not see her make that commitment to Jesus I had believed in my heart that she did not make it. It is not for me or you to decide which people get into Heaven, or which people do not. Jesus is the only way.

My wife has led many people to the Lord while working with the elderly in the hospitals and such. Their relatives never found out about it, but Jesus did. Jesus does not give up on anyone, even to his or her last breath on this earth. It is only Jesus. He is the Gate Keeper.

Chapter 10

Medical Records and Transcripts

Before this incident took place, I was a very healthy 47 year old male. I had regular physical checkups. Most of these checkups were because I was in the United States Air Force on active duty for 6 years and reserve duty for 14 years. I retired from the Reserves with a clean bill of health. The only problem I had after that was kidney stones in June of 2002, four years prior to this incident.

I went through the same procedure in 2002, for kidney stones as I did for this incident. The main difference was that this time I checked into the hospital the night before the operation. In June of 2002 I checked into the hospital that morning and came out in the afternoon of the same day. After the first treatment for kidney stones in 2002, I did not have any problems with kidney stones or any other illness for the next four years. I do not remember taking any sick leave for personal illness during this time.

The following is taken from the medical records we received from both hospitals. Getting these records was not easy because of the mistakes that were made by the hospitals and/or doctor, and the potential of a law suit. The doctor who made the mistakes made it hard for us to receive accurate reports. Finally, we had to get other doctors who worked on my case to give us the information. It was never our intention to sue the doctor or the hospital. We just wanted the official medical records to support the medical testimonies we had received from doctors, nurses, and other people who worked in the hospitals.

The other thing about these records is that it has been hard to get a medical professional to read what we have and interpret the medical jargon for the non-medical person, namely the readers of this book. We encountered resistance from people not wanting to go on record in translating the medical account. They just did not want to support in writing the number of mistakes that were made by the Urologist and hospital. Again, they did not want to be a part of any potential lawsuit in the future. So, the following is raw information that will have to be translated by the reader.

Excerpts of Information Taken From My Medical Records and Medical Transcripts

Preoperative Diagnosis: Left ureteral calculus and bilateral nephrolithiasis (Kidney stones) and pyelonephritis (urinary tract infection)

Postoperative Diagnosis: Left ureteral calculus and bilateral nephrolithiasis and pyelonephritis

Operation: Cystoscopy with retrograde pyelogram, push back of ureteral calculus and bilateral extracorporeal shock wave lithotripsy

Indications: This delightful 49-year-old gentleman (really 47-year-old) presented to the hospital with pyelonephritis and obstruction ureteral calculus. After 24 hours of antibiotic coverage with supplemental antibiotic administration in operation room, he presents at this time for definitive surgical intervention.

Findings: Obstructing calculus in the left ureter is pushed back in the renal pelvis, and a 24-cm 7-french double-J stent is left in place in the ureter and that calculus further targets and both kidneys were fragmented with difficulty. After 2400 shocks, the procedure was terminated and the patient was awakened and returned to the recovery room in satisfactory condition. There were no complications He tolerated the procedure well. This was from a May 6, 2006 report by the surgeon who performed the original operation.

Excerpts Taken From The Rest of the Medical Records and Medical Transcripts

- Larger amount of fluid resuscitation for hypertension
- Poorly responsive
- Move legs to pain
- very cool digits with cyanotic toes
- Acute renal failure
- Secondary to acute tubular necrosis oliguric
- Profound septic shock
- Prolonged Cardiac Arrest
- CPR one hour and 45 minutes
- Septic shock with urasepisis
- Respiratory failure
- Pulmonary infiltrates
- Edema versus adult respiratory distress Syndrome
- Post prolonged CPR
- Post cardiac arrest

• Prolonged resuscitation

• Fulminant sepsis

• Too numerous to count stone in right kidney

• Chest x-rays show the development of diffuse pulmonary edema

• Urine culture sent yesterday is growing greater than 100,000 colonies of E. coli.

• Doctor reports of spent a total of 1 hour and 45 min. total critical care time with the patient not including procedure

• Server sepsis

• Diagnosis of SIRS/Sepsis with hypotension, tachycardia, tachypnea, hypoxemia.

• High risk of disseminated intravascular coagulation.

• Cardiac arrest

• Urasepsis with E.Coli.

• Secondary renal shut down.

• Asystable

• Extubated

• Herodynamically Stable

• Shock liver

• Shock syndrome

• Hemodynamic stress

• On mechanical ventilation

• Paralytic ileus

- Multi-organ failure
- Critically ill
- Prognosis is poor
- Quniton Catheter and dialysis treatment (risk & Benefits)
- Risk for bleeding complication with ongoing DIC
- Clotting dialysis system given ongoing DIC
- Obstruction urinary stones
- Severely acidotic with a lactic acid as high as 16.
- Poorly responsive
- Requiring High Fi0 Moderate to servers patchy air space
- Opacities in the lungs bilaterally slightly increased. This is a word for progression of pneumonia.
- Very unfortunate critically ill patient.

After the recovery, I did receive some resistance from the doctor who had performed the operation in taking out a stint that was placed in my body. My wife had to call the doctor and state that she was going to take legal action if we did not receive an appointment to have the stint removed. We did receive an appointment for the next day and the doctor removed the stint.

I asked the doctor at this time what happened to cause my heart to stop. He said that I had a bad infection that he thought was taken care of with some really strong medicine. But for some reason the infection was not affected by the medicine that had been given to me. He said they had not checked prior to the operation if the medicine worked or not, and had assumed it did. It was not until five days later, that they found out from lab reports that the medicine did not have any effect on the infection.

At the time of the incident, the doctor did not know what was going wrong or why my vital organs were shutting down. The doctor told me that if they had not done everything correctly, I would have been dead. If they had done a procedure ten minutes earlier or ten minutes later, I would have been dead. I did ask him if I had died. He said my heart had stopped, and that every time it looked like it was going to start beating again, it would not. He said they worked on me about 1 hour and 30 minutes (Official record stated 1 hour and 45 minutes). I asked him if he saw this as a miracle and he said it was, and that I should go tell others the story. As you can read, there were a lot of things that went wrong with the procedures and with my body. But God healed all of them! Praise God!

Chapter 11

Jesus Wants All People Saved

What was Jesus doing when I got to Heaven? He was busy doing something that really surprised me. He was strategizing with some beings that were standing in a half circle facing Him.* He was communicating His plans to them of how to get more people on this earth to know Him as Lord and Savior.*

God is using everything that He can to get people to know Jesus as Lord and Savior.* He is looking for people on earth to work with Him in getting other people to know who He is.* I came to understand how much we are at war while I was in Heaven. Jesus is urging all of mankind to press into the Kingdom of God.* We are so very important to Him!* When I was in Heaven, I was connected to everything and everyone, and everything and everyone was connected to me. Because of this, I understood just how important we that are on earth are to Him. *

Heavenly Interventions

I say that I was surprised at what Jesus was doing because I believed that after He died on the cross and ascended into Heaven, there wouldn't be any need for such strategizing. However, when I look through the New Testament there is more than one occurrence, where

Jesus sends angels on what I call "heavenly interventions" to get people saved.*

For example, in Acts chapter 8, Phillip is sent to minister to the Ethiopian eunuch. In Acts chapter 9, Ananias is sent to Saul (Paul), and in Acts chapter 10, Peter is sent to bring salvation to Cornelius and his household. As soon as someone turns to God in his or her heart, Jesus is right there.* I tell others that there are many people in Heaven that we perhaps did not think would be there*. There are also those who we thought would be in Heaven, but are not.* As it says in Romans chapter 10, God is looking at a person's heart, not just what they say or do. *

Heaven is a place where everything is right and everyone has the right to be in a place of rightness.* Everything there is alive and everyone has a right to live with God forever.* I understood that is why we on earth are here. We are to tell others about Jesus so that they can go and be with GOD too.

The Army of God

There are two units in the army of God. There is a heavenly unit and an earthly unit, but they are the same army of God.* The heavenly unit is made up of the angels of God.* I saw how the heavenly unit worked. They understood whose government they belong to.* They understood whose Kingdom they work for.* When Jesus would communicate to them, they showed great AWE or respect.* I have not forgotten that moment. One of the other reasons I did not want to leave Heaven is because I wanted to be a part of that unit. I wanted to be with His creation that respected Him for who He is. He is the King of Kings and Lord of Lords. *

This respect and reverence for Jesus that I experienced in Heaven greatly affected me. I can remember telling my son in the hospital room, that I could not sing any songs any more that did not respect

Jesus as King. I witnessed how those heavenly creatures would bow when they came before the Lord and bow before they left Jesus, and then back out as they left.* They would not ever turn their back to Him. They left quickly to complete the assignments that He sent them on,* and I did not see any of them question anything He commanded them to do.* This heavenly unit was sent to fight in the heavenlies.* They were fighting evil spirits that belong to Satan's army*. I knew that it was prayer that determined these heavenly movements.* I will cover more about these two areas, prayer and angels, in later chapters.

Then, there was the earthly unit. *This is the one I was sent back to. I did not want to be a part of this one because I had already been a part of the heavenly unit. I had seen on earth the complete opposite of what the heavenly unit did. I had done on earth the complete opposite of what the heavenly unit does.

When Jesus told me to "Go Back", I knew within he was saying, "I need you on earth more than here," and I left as a soldier going to war.* I knew that it would be for a short time and that my life on this earth would be short*. If I stay here another 50 or 100 years, it is short compared to eternity. I have said to many people here on earth that I want to live to be at least 95. I want to be a part of this unit here on earth as long as I can. I know what the heart of God is. It is to get people saved. It is to get people to live with Him forever.*

God's Army On Earth

While in Heaven, I came to understand what the earthly unit looks like. First of all, this unit is composed of people who love God with all their being.* These are they that say Jesus is Lord and Savior,* not just Savior of their lives, but also Lord of their lives. They know they are sent to tell others of Jesus. They know who sent them.* They have come to an understanding of His authority and whose authority they have.* They know there is a war going on with Satan and his fallen angels.* They know their weapons and use them in battles they encounter.* They have a great understanding of whose government and kingdom they are under and belong to.* They spend a lot of time with the Father in His Word and in prayer.* They are able to hear His voice when He commands them to do something*. They understand that when Jesus or the Father through the Holy Spirit asks them to do something for the Kingdom, it is a command and not a request.* These have come to know their purpose on this earth and accept it.* They know that they are to get people to know Jesus as Lord and Savior at all cost. They are willing to lose their lives here on earth for Him.* They know that they are part of a bigger army and have a God that will always be with them.*

I came to understand that I was not being sent out alone with a heavy load.* I understood that someone prayed me into the Kingdom of God. I also understood that God used both the heavenly and the earthly units to accomplish that in my life, and I know that He did the same thing for others who are reading this that are saved. If you are reading this and are not saved, God is having the heavenly unit fight on your behalf. He is using me and others in the earthly unit on your behalf. I say to you: "Stop right now, and ask Jesus to be your Lord and Savior. Say the following prayer and know how much God loves you."

Prayer For Salvation

I know I have sinned. I am sorry for my sin. I believe Jesus that you died on the cross for my sin. I now receive you as my own Savior and Lord. With your help, Jesus, I will try to please you every day of my life. I will be a great soldier of honor in your army, in Jesus's name, Amen.

Chapter 12

Over 600 Heard of Dean's Miracle Through Email

The following emails were sent announcing my condition. This email went out to people I worked with or for at the time of the incident. It was also sent out to other departments throughout King County and the City of Seattle and to many of the different social agencies that I had worked with. In all, it can be said that this incident was announced to over 600 people. When I showed up back to work a month and a half later, people would say it was a miracle. I would then agree that it was a miracle performed by Jesus Christ and our Father God.

First Email

May 10, 2006 Hi Everyone,

This is a Wednesday update on Dean Braxton, beloved Manager of Juvenile Drug Court, and Treatment Court. As most all of you know by now, Dean had emergency surgery for kidney stones last Friday, May 5th, at St. Francis Hospital in Federal Way. Due to an infection and many other complications following the surgery, Dean's heart, kidneys and other vital organs began to shut down and he was placed on life support. He was transported on Saturday morning to Tacoma General Hospital ICU. He remains on life support, including a ventilator, 24/7 kidney dialysis, etc. He has made some progress in recovery and response over the past 3 days. He is receiving excellent care by the ICU medical team.

Currently, medical staffers are monitoring his heart, kidneys, and other functions and have addressed the white blood count problem that was discovered yesterday. His levels are returning to a more normal white count. They have had to increase his oxygen levels, however. This means he cannot breathe on his own. Although he cannot speak due to the ventilator, he is responding with facial expressions and tears when his wife and elderly parents speak with him. That is a good sign regarding his brain functioning and the wonderful spirit inside of Dean. We are continuing to pray for his complete recovery.

Dean's wife, Marilyn Braxton, would like to thank everyone for his or her kind visits, cards, telephone calls and other expressions of care and concern. She would like to request, however, that during this very critical time that Dean is on life-support, that all visits to Dean would be put on hold and all telephone calls to her would also be limited. Ycaza and Hazel from the 4Cs Coalition will be the main point people that I will be keeping updated through, as they are both very close to Marilyn and Dean and talking to her often.

We have arranged to have some food and beverages delivered to the family this week and we will keep you all posted on what is needed along the way. During this time of crisis, the family is spending very little time at home, so the needs are somewhat different.

Thank you for your loving care and concern, your offers of support and your continued prayers for Dean's healing and recovery. It is encouraging to all of us and to his family.

I will be in touch again soon,

Susie

Second Email

May 11, 2006 Good Morning Everyone,

This is a Thursday morning update on Dean Braxton: Marilyn Braxton reports that Dean is improving significantly at all levels. They are having conversations and other communication that shows to you the level of his improvement! Many miracles are unfolding and the ICU team at Tacoma General Hospital continues to be doing a superb job of caring for him.

Marilyn, Dean and their extended family want to express their continued gratefulness for your loving support, prayers and concern. They are encouraged by Dean's progress and want to pass along that encouragement to you. There is a road ahead to recovery, and it is great to report his movement along this road!

Dean will remain in ICU for a time because of the many issues involved in his care. I will keep you posted as I receive word from Marilyn through Hazel of the 4Cs Coalition about Dean's status and if he is moved to a regular room at the hospital.

Susie

Third Email

May 12, 2006 Good Afternoon Everyone,

This is a very encouraging update regarding Dean Braxton from his wife Marilyn. Over the past 24-30 hours, Dean has been making a remarkable recovery, nothing short of miraculous, given the health crisis he has faced since last Friday, just 1 week ago.

While he is still in the ICU at Tacoma General Hospital, he is improving by the hour, and is able to converse with his family and the medical staff. His doctors are in awe of how quirky he has responded to treatment and how well he is doing.

Marilyn and the immediate family are with him much of the time and wanted to express their gratitude to all of you for your thoughts, prayers, and concerns for Dean. They are encouraged and grateful for the miracle of his recovery process. It is unclear at this time how much longer Dean will be in ICU. There are many factors that must be addressed before he would move to a regular hospital room.

The family is still in need of gift cards for food. I will be taking a couple to them this evening. I would welcome any further donations any time during next week. I will be back in my office late Monday afternoon and part of Tuesday.

Thank again for your concern, prayers and support. On behalf of the Drug Court/Treatment Court Teams,

Susie

Fourth Email

May 15, 2006 Hello Everyone,

I just spoke to Marilyn Braxton and Dean has been moved out of ICU, although he is still is at Tacoma General. He is progressing every hour; she stated that he took a walk down the hall yesterday! She expressed her thanks for all the outpouring of love and support... And the doctors continue to be amazed at the rapid pace of recovery. We are all encouraged keep the positive thoughts and prayers coming...

Susie

Fifth Email

May 16, 2006

Hi... Wasn't sure if you were included in yesterday's email from Margaret, Manager of Reclaiming Futures. Now that the team is back from their conference, Margaret or Mark will most likely provide the update information. I was out sick yesterday, but spoke with Marilyn last evening. Dean is improving by the hour. It continues to be a miracle... Even to the doctors. At this point, he may be able to go home in a few days. He will still have recovering to do, but is almost well enough to do that at home! It's pretty much a WOW, isn't it!

Thanks for your thoughts and prayers for him,

Susie

Chapter 13

What Jesus Told Me About Our Churches

When I was with Jesus, He looked at me and downloaded a great amount of information into my spirit-man. The only way I can explain this process is it is like a computer receiving information or being programmed with information from another source, what we call downloading information into a computer. That is how Jesus communicates information to all of us. Most people do not hear an audible voice from Jesus. Most of the time we receive information from Jesus like a computer being downloaded with information all at once. This is the same way he communicates with all beings in Heaven. Sharing information about my experience in Heaven and what God said to me is like my taking apart a whole picture given to me at one time and giving it out in pieces to others. Now, I want to let you know what Jesus downloaded into me about the churches here on earth and in the United States.

Two Spirits in the Church

First, He let me know that there are two spirits or attitudes in our churches today.* Both of these spirits or attitudes are found in Revelation 3:7-21. He said to me that these spirits are not in only one denomination* or one kind of church building, the way I used to think before I went to Heaven. In the past I believed I was always in the "right" denomination and others were not. Whether I was with the Church of God in Christ, Southern Baptist, Assembly of God, Four Square or many non-denominational churches, I always believed my denomination was the right one. I believed we had the right spirit or attitude in that denomination.

Jesus told me that His church is not one denomination or another. I came to realize that there are many things that we, church-goers, believe in that do not get us into Heaven or keep us out. They instead keep us from helping others come to know Jesus as Lord and Savior. Chapter 10 in Romans contains the scripture that tells EVERYONE what they must do to enter the gates of Heaven.* If a person will confess Jesus as Lord and believe that He was raised from the dead, Jesus will come into their heart and fill it with an overwhelming love for God and for others.* God's presence in us causes changes in our thinking and actions, not a denomination or its traditions.

We Are One Body

Believers in Christ do meet in different buildings, but God sees everyone who has accepted Jesus as Lord and Savior as His church.* He wants each of us to belong to a local body of believers so we can build each other up for the work He has set before us,* and so that we can fellowship with others in His kingdom. However, there are not any denominational lines in Heaven. The many old jokes about denominations in Heaven are just jokes and are not true.

At the time I am writing this book, my wife and I do belong to a local body of believers. The name of the church is By His Word Christian Center in Tacoma, Washington. I came to understand that it is part of the government of God, as a local body of those who believe in Jesus as the Son of God and have made Him Lord and Savior of their lives.*These are people that believe that God the Father sent His Son into the world to save it, to save you, and to save people.* They believe the Holy Spirit, Jesus, and the Father are one, and that there is only one true God,* the one who made man*, not a man- made God.*This kind of true believers in Christ can be found in all church bodies, no matter the denomination or non-denomination.

Jesus said that there are two spirits in EVERY body of believers. Some bodies may have more of one spirit than others, but both spirits can be found in the same body of believers. This changed how I look at churches all over this world. I came to know that every building that holds a church meeting has both of these spirits in it. One of these spirits can be stronger than the other in the same meeting, but both may be present.

Jesus is not happy when we esteem one church's believing body over another church's believing body. We are all part of the same church, His church. Jesus told me that He has His children in many of these believing bodies, and that they may meet in a number of different buildings and in different denominations. Everyone who believes that Jesus is the Christ has been fathered by God (1John 5:1).* He wanted me to know that these two spirits are in ALL church bodies, no matter what the denomination or non-denomination so we should stop tearing each other down. He is still working with all of us. He wants us to follow His Government or Kingdom rules on how to confront, correct, and deal with each other.*

The First Spirit

The first spirit Jesus told me about is found in Revelation 3:8-12. It was found in the church of Philadelphia.

REVELATION 3:8-12 (NKJV)

> "I know your works. See, I have set before you an open door, and no one can shut it, for you have a little strength, have kept my word, and have not denied My name. Indeed I will make those of the synagogue of Satan, who say they are Jews and are not, but lie—indeed I will make them come and worship before your feet, and to know that I have loved you. Because you have kept My command to persevere, I also will keep you from the hour of trial which shall come upon the whole world, to test those who dwell on the earth. Behold, I am coming quickly! Hold fast what you have, that no one may take your crown. He who overcomes, I will make him a pillar in the temple of My God, and he shall go out no more. I will write on him the name of My God and the name of the city of My God, the New Jerusalem, which comes down out of heaven from My God. And I will write on him My new name."

This spirit seeks to serve others first.* Those who have this spirit keep God's Word at all cost.* They have not denied His Name.* They also know His Word is the Word of perseverance* in which He will keep them from the hour of testing.* Those who have this spirit know in their heart that He is coming quickly. They understand that because the time is short before Jesus returns they want to see more people saved. They are holding fast to what they know.*Those that have this spirit have a crown that no one can take from them. They can give it away, but no one can take it.* They are truly overcoming all that they face on this earth.* They will be made a pillar in God's temple and will not go out from the temple of God.* They will have the name of God written on them along with the name of the city of God on them*. This spirit is in all churches that believe in Jesus Christ as Lord and Savior.

The Second Spirit

The second spirit or attitude that Jesus told me was found in all churches is found in Revelation 3:15-21. It was dominant in the Laodicea church.

REVELATION 3:15-21 (NKJV)

> "I know your works, that you are neither cold nor hot. I could wish you were cold or hot. So then, because you are lukewarm, and neither cold nor hot, will I vomit you out of My mouth. Because you say, 'I am rich, have become wealthy, and have need of nothing'—and do not know that you are wretched, miserable, poor, blind, and naked. I counsel you to buy from Me gold refined in the fire, that you may be rich; and white garments, that you may be clothed, that the shame of your nakedness may not be revealed; and anoint your eyes with eye salve, that you may see. As many as I love, I rebuke and chasten. Therefore be zealous and repent. Behold, I stand at the door and knock. If anyone hears My voice and opens the door, I will come in to him and dine with him, and he with Me. To him who overcomes I will grant to sit with Me on My throne, as I also overcame and sat down with My Father on His throne."

This is the spirit I did not want. At the time of this incident I believed that any church that met in a traditional building was the church at Laodicea. I was pastoring a small home church at the time and was very happy there. I had been a part of a traditional church for a number of years as you have already read, and most of those years, as an assistant pastor. Because of some of the experiences I had in those churches I no longer wanted to have anything to do with them. I felt that the older the denomination, the more dominant was this Laodicean spirit. But, as I stated before, Jesus changed that kind of thinking for me. I know

now that it has nothing to do with a building or a denomination, but it has everything to do with each person's heart.*

This Laodicean spirit is neither cold nor hot.* It does not work for God. These people who call themselves believers in Jesus are not on the side of God. Jesus said He wished they were either cold or hot. Because they are lukewarm He is going to spit (Greek: vomit) them out of His mouth.* They that have this spirit say they are rich, wealthy and need nothing.* They may not say it out loud so that others can hear them, but in their heart they believe this. Jesus said they do not know they are really wretched, miserable, poor, blind, and naked.* Their problem is that God knows their heart, and He knows which spirit they have.*

Jesus also goes on to tell them to buy gold that has been refined by fire from Him.* He wants them to be truly rich. He wants them to have white garments so they can clothe themselves.* He does not want the shame of their nakedness to be revealed. He wants them to have their eyes to be opened so they can see.* Because HE LOVES THEM, he reproves and disciplines them who have this spirit.* He wants them to be zealous and repent from this spirit. Jesus is knocking on the door to their spirit, waiting for them to open their spirit to Him.* He wants to come into their spirit and dine with them and them with Him. Those who repent and overcome this lukewarm state will sit down with Jesus on His throne.

I came to understand that there are those who are lukewarm in every church, no matter what building they meet in or what denomination they belong to, He is reaching out to them. Do not be deceived like I was. He loves them so much that He will keep knocking until they open up or die. I was one of those lukewarm people for a long time, and He did not give up on me. He does not want us to give up on the others either.

The Church Can Change Our Nations

The other thing that Jesus communicated to me while I was in Heaven was "How the church down here on earth goes, so does a nation."* If we see a problem in our nation we must first look at our churches. He really does want His people, who are called by His name to humble themselves, pray, seek His face and turn from their individual wicked ways.* If His people will do this, their nation will turn around.* We that believe in Jesus as Lord and Savior, can change our nations whether it is the United States, Peru, France, England, Canada, China, Uganda, Israel, or any another nation.* He wants us to know it can happen. We can change the nations by starting with our churches.

2 CHRONICLES 7:14 (NKJV)

> "If My people who are called by My name will humble themselves, and pray and seek My face, and turn from their wicked ways, then I will hear from heaven, and will forgive their sin and heal their land."

Chapter 14

What God Does With Our Prayers

2 CORINTHIANS 5:8 (NKJV)

> "...to be absent from the body and to be present with the Lord."

It was great to be traveling to where Jesus is. I was moving very fast. I did not see anyone when I left. I was not looking for anyone else but Jesus. I knew where I was going. On the way back to my body I did see demons in that thick blackness that surrounds our galaxies. As I got close to the hospital, I saw the doctors and nurse working on me in the hospital room. However, when I left my body, I was not looking back. I knew where to go and no one had to tell me where to go.* I did not need any direction. I did not need an angel taking me. I knew I was going home and I was to be at the feet of Jesus.

Now as I said, I was moving very very fast, faster than we as humans can even imagine. As 2 Corinthians says, I was absent from my body, and I was in the presence of my Lord.* I was moving faster than it takes you to read the next sentence. I was absent from my body and in the presence of my Lord. If I were to die right now, I would be in Heaven in a twinkling of an eye. Yet, the prayers of people that were praying for me and others were moving faster than I was*. They were like shooting stars passing me. All I saw as they went by me were balls that looked like fire with a tail of light that looked like fire. I saw prayers as I was going to Heaven and prayers as I was coming back to the hospital on earth. I was moving in a river of prayers going to Heaven. The prayers that were close to me were for me. The prayers that were farther away were for other people. Just think, if you were praying at the time I left my body to go to Heaven, I saw your prayers pass me by. They passed me as if I were standing still. Yet, to be absent from my body was to be in the presence of my Lord.

Two Types of Prayers

I knew there were two types of prayers passing me. One type of prayer was prayers from people that had prayed a prayer and understood the authority they had when they prayed that prayer.* They were praying in faith from their hearts.* They were praying according to a verse in the Bible that they understood the meaning of.* They were praying the will of God for me and others.* So when they prayed that prayer, they knew in their heart what it was supposed to do. And they knew that God would answer the prayer with His power.* John tells us about this kind of prayer.

1 JOHN 5:14-15 (NKJV)

> "Now this is the confidence that we have in Him, that if we ask anything according to His will, He hears us. And if we know that He hears us, whatever we ask, we know that we have the petitions that we have asked of Him."

Now I had no problem with this kind of prayer. We are told to pray His will here on earth in Matthew 6:10.* I had studied to know His will according to the Bible, so this prayer did not surprise me.

This was the also the kind of prayer that my wife was praying, along with my children and others. It was God's will for me to come back to this earth. Since it was His will it was answered. But also remember my wife's sacrifice and battle to get that outcome.* That was God's will too.

The other prayer was a surprise to me. It was a prayer that I never thought existed. This was one of the box-blowing moments for me (think outside of the box). It was a prayer that people had prayed when they really did not have the full understanding of what they were praying. They did not doubt what they were praying. They just did not understand the full impact of what they had asked for. They were on the right track to understanding the will of God in an area, but did not fully understand it yet. They had faith in what they prayed, not really understanding what they were fully praying for. *

Yet, God honored the prayer as if they understood the power of what they had asked.

Again, these people did not doubt what they were praying for, but had faith for all they understood. I like to say that they believed they were praying for something that would produce a bang as big as a firecracker and God would honor their prayer as a nuclear bomb. He was going to answer the prayer as if they understood the full impact of what they were praying about. You see this best in little children. I have seen a child pray for something and as far as they know, it is done. They may know very little about the Bible, but they do know about God. You can find this prayer in Ephesians.

EPHESIANS 3:20 (NKJV)

"Now to Him who is able to do exceedingly abundantly above all that we ask or think, according to the power that works in us."

Where Our Prayers Go

Now as I said before, I went to the feet of Jesus and stopped there. The prayers went straight to the throne and the Father. Not only did they go to the Father God, they went inside of Him.* To try to understand this you will have to understand that the throne of God is not a seat. It is a place. Well, more than that, He is the Throne. I will cover the Throne of God in this book later. But for now, I need to continue with what happens to the prayers we pray. There were millions upon millions of prayers entering the Father. Our prayers became Him and He became our prayers. I saw these lights of prayers like shooting stars entering the Father. I came to understand that He answers our prayers with Himself. *

At first, when I came back to earth and someone asked me about prayers I had a hard time telling them what I saw. This again, was outside of my boxes. I remembered praying to the Father and asking Him for the words to explain this to others. How do I explain seeing the prayers of people here on earth enter God? When He directed me to Exodus, I found the answer to explain the prayers going into the Father.

EXODUS 3:13-14 (NKJV)

> "Then Moses said to God, "Indeed, when I come to the children of Israel and say to them, 'The God of your fathers has sent me to you,' and they say to me, 'What is His name?' what shall I say to them?" And God said to Moses, "I AM WHO I AM." And He said, "Thus you shall say to the children of Israel, 'I AM has sent me to you."

The Lord says here: I AM. HE IS THE ANSWER TO OUR PRAYERS! He does answer our prayers with Himself. Why did He come? Why did He come to the children of Israel? God tells us in Exodus 3:7-9 why He came.

EXODUS 3:7-9 (NKJV)

"And the LORD said: I have surely seen the oppression of My people who are in Egypt, and have heard their cry because of their taskmasters, for I know their sorrows. So I have come down to deliver them out of the hand of the Egyptians, and to bring them up from that land to a good and large land, to a land flowing with milk and honey, to the place of the Canaanites and the Hittites and the Amorites and the Perizzites and the Hivites and the Jebusites. Now therefore, behold, the cry of the children of Israel has come to Me, furthermore, and I have also seen the oppression with which the Egyptians oppress them."

The Israelites were praying for a deliverer, a savior, and a healer. The prayers went into the Father God and He became their answer. He became their deliverer, their savior, and their healer. He is our answer to any prayer that we have prayed to Him. He is our savior, joy, peace, righteousness, and so on. Right now just say it, "God is my answer to any problem I have and He wants to be!"

Our God Is!

Our God truly is the answer to our prayers, which is why we call Him:

- JEHOVAH-JIREH: Jehovah will see; i.e., will provide, the name given by Abraham to the scene of his offering up the ram which was caught in the thicket on Mount Moriah. The expression is, "The Lord Provides." It is said to this day, "In the mountain of the Lord provision will be made." "In the mount of the Lord it shall be seen," has been regarded as equal to the saying, "Man's extremity is God's opportunity." (Gen. 22:8, 14)

- **Jehovah-Nissi:** Jehovah my banner, the title given by Moses to the altar which he erected on the hill on the top of which he stood with uplifted hands while Israel prevailed over their enemies the Amalekites (Ex. 17:15 Lord is my Banner)

- **Jehovah-Shalom:** Yahweh is peace. This was the name given by Gideon to the altar he built at Ophra, in allusion to the word spoken to him by the Lord, "Peace be unto thee" (Judges 6:24)

- **Jehovah-Shammah:** Jehovah is there, the symbolical title given by Ezekiel to Jerusalem, which was seen by him in a vision. The name of the city from that day forward will be The Lord Is There. It was a type of the gospel Church. (Ezek. 48:35)

- **Jehovah-Tsidckenu:** Jehovah our righteousness, rendered in the Authorized Version, "The LORD our righteousness," a title given to the Messiah. Judah will enjoy safety and Israel will live in security. This is the name he will go by: The Lord has provided us with justice. And also to Jerusalem (Jeremiah 23:6, 33:16) whatever the need you have, He is the answer. The Bible tells us this and it is true.

Prayers From the Heart

Jesus downloaded information into me about prayers. I understood that our prayers must come from our heart.* Our God is a heart God, and He is looking for us to talk to Him from our heart.* I do not have the words yet to describe this, but our prayers become substances.* What kind of substance? I do not have the words to describe it. They only become substances if we are praying to God from our heart. He hears us if we are praying from our heart. This is why most little children receive their requests.* In Romans 10:9 God is looking at the heart.

ROMANS 10:9 (NKJV)

"that if you confess with your mouth the Lord Jesus and believe in your heart that God raised Him from the dead, you will be saved."

He hears your heart. He understands your heart.* He only hears prayers from the heart.* Some ask, "What if your heart is wrong when you pray?" The Holy Spirit will let you know.* It is up to you to listen to Him. He will also help you to pray from your heart.* The Holy Spirit came to help us do a lot of things the way God wants them done.* Prayer is one of those things. Read Luke 11:1-13 to understand what happens to the prayers we pray from the heart.

LUKE 11:13 (NKJV)

"If you then, being evil, know how to give good gifts to your children, how much more will your heavenly Father give the Holy Spirit to those who ask Him!"

MATTHEW 7:11 (NKJV)

"If you then, being evil, know how to give good gifts to your children, how much more will your Father who is in heaven give good things to those who ask Him!"

People have asked, "How do I know if I am praying His will?" My reply to them is, "Ask Him to help you pray from your heart." *I know He hears you because that is His will. You can read that again in 1 John 5:14-15. Then pray from the heart. After you ask Him from your heart, you do not have to ask Him again*. He heard you. God is not hard of hearing or remembering, but we pray to Him as if He is.

I understood that our prayers do not need to be repeated if they are asked from the heart, and that our Father does not forget a prayer that is asked from the heart. We may forget our prayers, but He does not. A person asked me one time, "What if I did not pray right? Do I have to ask it again?" I replied, "You can if you want, but God listens to your heart." If you are asking from the heart He hears you. You have your request. Now thank Him.*

Prayers Don't Have a Shelf Life

Another thing I came to understand about prayer is that if it is a prayer from the heart, it does not have a shelf life.* God does not forget your prayers. He remembers them until they are answered. It could be within minutes, hours, days, years, or even longer. But, your prayers do not expire. There is not an expiration date on them.

This means that those prayers you keep on praying over and over for someone to get saved, He heard you the first time, and as soon as that person turns their heart toward God, God will be there to meet that person. All you need to do now is thank Him. He wants your loved ones to be saved more than you do.* Remember, the Father gave his Son, Jesus, so that they could be saved.* So thank Him for hearing your prayer and for answering your prayer. It does not matter if you see it answered here on earth or when you are in Heaven.* Wherever you are, you will rejoice.

My mother did not make Jesus her Lord and Savior over her life until ten years after my grandmother Mary, her mother, had died. I know when my mother made that step, my grandmother Mary rejoiced over my mother's salvation.

Some of you that are reading this right now are answers to a prayer that someone prayed a long time ago. Some of you are an answer to a prayer that some great, great, great, great grandparent prayed. They prayed for a great, great, great, great grandchild to know Jesus as Lord and Savior.* And since, there is no expiration date, when you turned your heart to God, their prayer was answered. Some of you have prayers that were prayed over you by someone a long time ago that God is still waiting to answer. You just need to get your heart right. Ask Jesus to help you.

Here is one more thing I must say about what I learned about prayer. Our prayers cause movement in the Kingdom of God. Jesus is strategizing by how we pray.* In the Bible we can read that we are to pray for the Lord to send laborers into His harvest in Matthew 9:37-38.*

Jesus Giving Out Orders

When I saw Jesus strategizing, He knelt down to the ground and put His hand out pointing at the ground and the ground rose up and became a city. What city? I could not tell you. I just knew it was an earthly city. He pointed at areas in the city and looked up at a being (angel). They would bow, and back out fast. I knew He had given them instruction on what to do. I knew that Jesus had received information about a situation on earth that the Father had gotten from someone praying here on earth and gave that information to Jesus at the same moment He had received the information. Then Jesus saw what the Father wanted and gave that information to the angel, and he would leave to go to the earth. The angel or angels would carry out the orders that were given to them by Jesus.

You can also read about this in Daniel 10:12. I know that my wife put this into action from earth when she prayed the will of God. She acted on Matthew 6:10 and Luke 11:2

MATTHEW 6:10 (NKJV)

> "Your kingdom come. Your will be done on earth as it is in heaven."

LUKE 11:2 (NKJV)

> "So He said to them, "When you pray, say: Our Father in heaven, Hallowed be Your name. Your kingdom come. Your will be done On earth as it is in heaven."

We are told to pray for the will of Heaven here on earth. This is what I saw when I was there. God's will was being done in Heaven as it was to be done here on earth.

Another thing that must be said loud and clear is that we have the only God who hears prayer.* Sometimes we act as if there are a number of gods in Heaven, and ours is just one of them. This is not true. I saw only one God, and He was not sharing His Throne with anyone else*, not Mohammed, Buddha, or any other so-called religious figure. Now, the Father God who sits on the Throne and Jesus, the son of God, were the only ones receiving praise from the creation of God in Heaven. No other being or creation of God was getting, receiving or giving praise to any other but the Father and Jesus.

There is only one God who can hear our prayers and answer them all around the world. No other so-called god can. We must understand that there is only one God, and one God who hears prayers. WE MUST BELIEVE THAT! As I said before, we pray to the God who made man, not a god made by man.

Chapter 15

I Saw God the Father On His Throne and His Love For Us!

As I said earlier, I saw the prayers people were praying for me and the prayers of others entering God the Father on His Throne as I was on my way to Heaven to be with Jesus. I want to attempt to describe Father God as I saw Him there in Heaven.

God, the Father, is, as the Bible says, a Spirit. He is pure SPIRIT. He is pure LOVE. He is pure LIFE, and He is pure LIGHT. That is who He is. If only we could understand that in our interpretation of the Bible. I tell people that this understanding of who God is, gave me a better understanding of what I read in the Bible. I connect everything that God does back to who He is: Love, Life and Light. He cannot come to us in any other way than what He is. All that He does comes out of who He is. He is love, just like John tells us in the Bible. He is the true Spirit and we must worship Him in spirit and in truth.* He is pure light that is still expanding. He is life.

In Heaven, I heard all of creation, except those who have been redeemed, refer to the Father God as the WORD.* He is His Word and His Word is Him. They would say, "The Word said..."

Now, those of us who are redeemed would call Him Father.* We are truly His children and we refer to Him as Father. This is good news. We who are redeemed are the only ones who call Him Father.

What Does the Father Look Like?

I have had this question asked many times, "What does the Father look like?" They ask if He looks human. My words are He is vast. He is very vast.* The word "big" does not come close to describing what I saw or experienced. The angels that fly around Him saying, "Holy, Holy, Holy", are very small compared to God.* He has the form of a human, or better yet, we have the form of God.* We look like Him. We were made after His likeness. I really cannot put my thinking around Him. He is large, huge, vast, infinite, enormous, immeasurable, unrestricted, unrestrained, never-ending, endless, without end, free, and at liberty to be God. I like to say the word "vast", mostly because the word comes out of my mouth in such a way that there is no ending. I really have not found words in English to describe God. I have no thoughts that can even seem to grasp what I saw. When I try to put Him in my thinking, I can't. If I think of the beginning of Him, I lose the end, and if I think of the end, I lose the beginning. One time, I thought on this for a little while and knew if I kept trying to place God inside of my thinking, I was going to end up with a headache. So I just don't try it anymore. You that know Jesus as Lord and Savior, you will see Him and understand what I am saying. All I can say is that He is vast.

There is no end to God the Father. He is bright like Jesus with many colors coming off of Him.* Jesus and the Father God light up everything. They do not let any darkness in Heaven. None at all! Every being there has God the Father and Jesus inside of them. God lives outside of every being and inside every being. Every being shines because of the Father God and Jesus. They are the light within every living being and creature. Darkness has nowhere to hide.

I feel that I am coming way short in telling you about the Father. There seems to be no words that are fitting or that describe accurately what I saw. Jesus was easier to describe only because He has a new body.

We that know Jesus as Lord and Savior will someday have that same body He has.

The Father's Throne

I saw the Father God sitting on the Throne, and again, one of my thought boxes was blown up. He was sitting on the Throne and yet, He is the Throne.* As I said earlier, He had these colors that were radiating from Him, more colors than I have ever seen or experienced. These colors were alive. Everything that comes from God the Father is alive. Before the Throne, there were an uncountable number of heavenly creatures giving God praise. Later, I will go into more details of this praise before the Throne of God.

What did the Throne of God look like? This is what I saw: God was vast and the Throne was God, and God was the Throne. He was in the midst of the Throne and connected to the Throne. Where He was, the Throne was there. The Throne was bright and looked like a cloud.* I had always believed God was sitting on a chair, but that was not so. This is one of my thought boxes that was blown up. The throne instead looked like a cloud.

What I experienced about the Throne was that God the Father was and has never been separated from the Throne.* When I talk about the Throne, it has been hard for me to take in all that I experienced before the Throne of God. God says in Isaiah that, "Heaven is My Throne and the earth is My footstool."

ISAIAH 66:1-2 (NKJV)

"Thus says the Lord: "Heaven is My throne, and the earth is My footstool. Where is the house that you will build Me? And where is the place of My rest? "For all those things My hand has made, and all those things exist," says the Lord."

ACTS 7:48-50 (NKJV)

"However, the Most High does not dwell in temples made with hands, as the prophet says: "Heaven is My throne, and

> earth is My footstool. What house will you build for Me? says the Lord, "Or what is the place of My rest? Has My hand not made all these things?"

MATTHEW 5:34 (NKJV)

> "But I say to you, do not swear at all: neither by heaven, for it is God's throne."

This Throne which was God Himself is all I could come back with to tell others of what I saw. The Throne of God is not what I used to believe it was. I only could say to myself after seeing God on the Throne, in the midst of the Throne, and being the Throne, "Who could make a Throne for God, but God?"* And it was not like what a human would make.

Our Father's Love For Us

As I looked at the Throne, I saw how much the Father loves us. I knew that Jesus loved us so much, but to see the Father's love for us—WOW! I looked into His eyes. When I did, all I could think was, "I wonder how many universes you could place in His eyes." But out of all that I saw, what really stood out to me was the love that He has for each and every one of us on earth.*

I came to understand that every time we take a breath of air, the Father God is saying, "I love you."* The only reason air is here, is for you. There is no other reason that the air is here. How many times in a day do you take a breath of air? Whatever the number is, that is how many times God is telling you that He loves you. Hear Him as you breathe say, "I Love you."

We Are All Number One

Before the Throne of God I understood that there is no number two in God's eyes.* Everyone is number one. There is no one taking the place of number two, three, four, five, six, seven, eight, nine, or whatever before God. There is only number one, and everyone is number one to Him. Everyone is first in line with Him. There is no difference even here on earth. If you know Jesus as Lord and Savior, you are number one to Him. As the Bible says, we are the apple of His eye.

PSALM 17:8 (NKJV)

> "Keep me as the apple of Your eye; Hide me under the shadow of Your wings"
>
> Zechariah 2:8 (NKJV)
>
> "For thus says the LORD of hosts: "He sent Me after glory, to the nations which plunder you; for he who touches you touches the apple of His eye."

I came to know how valuable we are to Him*:

JOHN 3:16-17 (NKJV)

> "For God so loved the world that He gave His only begotten Son, that whoever believes in Him should not perish but have everlasting life. For God did not send His Son into the world to condemn the world, but that the world through Him might be saved."

Chapter 16

Worship Before the Throne of God

When I saw the Father God sitting on His Throne, there were an uncountable number of heavenly creatures there giving God praise. I was on my hands and knees when I looked at the Throne of God, and this is what I saw. I was far and yet I was near the Throne of God. Some of the beings that were around the Throne had been human beings from earth and others were heavenly beings. Between them and the Throne was something like water. John said in Revelation that it was like a crystal sea.* It looks like crystal, but it is not. It is something like water but not really. The closest I can come to describing this water-like substance is by calling it water. But again, it is like water but it is very much alive.

Now after this Crystal-like Sea there was another liquid under the Throne of God. The Throne hovers over this liquid and this liquid was also alive. It had a different thickness to it compared to the Crystal-like Sea. These two liquids flowed through each other, but did not overlap or blend or bleed into each other. They stayed very much separate. I have not found the words to really describe the beauty of both of these water-like liquids. All I can say is that they were alive and they each had a personality. Throughout Heaven there are other water-like liquids that are alive and have a fun personality.

When I was in Heaven there always seemed to be a sound of praise and worship. I came to understand that true worship is doing God's will. So in the atmosphere there was always what seemed to be like a musical sound. It was going on all the time and yet it was like no other sound that I know of. It was more than just hearing it. It was like you experienced it. The closest I can come to describing it is to liken it to the vibrations you might feel from a drum beat or from the bass coming from a car next to yours. This praise was always there in the atmosphere.

There was also a sound of praise and worship you could hear. Just before I saw what was happening before the Throne of God, all of what we would call sound, stopped.* It was quiet. Everything got really quiet. There was no noise at all. I came to know what quiet is. We always have noise going on around us here on earth. Even when we think it is quiet, there is always some sound going on around us. At that moment I did not hear a thing.

The Heavenly Worship Leader

The next thing I saw was one of the beings before the Throne rising up from a kneeling position. This being rose up like an elevator rising up from the bottom floor to the top slowly. This being was so beautiful. This being looked as if it were a woman but I knew it was not. It was a good hundred stories or higher. When it reached its highest point, this being raised its arms over its head to the full extent and extended its fingers out wide. The color of this being was light blue, like the sky on a sunny day. It seemed as if you could see through this being, but it was hard to tell because the rainbow colors radiating from God entered into this being.

After this being had finished rising, it opened its mouth and broke the silence that was taking place. It started to sing in a language I understood but I knew was not an earthly language. This language seemed to be this being's own language, but still I understood it. The sound that came out of its mouth was beautiful and yet, it was just one note. It came from the innermost part of its being. This being seemed to be making music within itself.* This is how all the beings there in Heaven produce music.

Musical Instruments Inside "The Being"

After being back on earth someone asked me about the music in Heaven. I told them about how I heard and saw music coming out of the beings in Heaven. After telling this to a person for the first time, I said within myself, "Dean, you have really gone off." But I knew I had to tell what I saw, whether people believed me or not. Whether I had believed this before or not, I had to tell the truth since they had asked. I had never heard anyone tell me that the angels in Heaven had instruments inside of themselves. That was the first time I said something that I had not known was in the Bible, but it would not be the last time. Later, I found out that Lucifer, now Satan, was created with instruments inside him.

EZEKIEL 28:13 (NKJV)

> "You were in Eden, the garden of God; Every precious stone was your covering: The sardius, topaz, and diamond, Beryl, onyx, and jasper, Sapphire, turquoise, and emerald with gold. The workmanship of your timbrels and pipes was prepared for you on the day you were created. (*KJV reads: IN THEE in the day that thou wast created.)*

Timbrels or tabrets: Greek word toph, Pronunciation: tofe Definition: 1) timbrel, tambourine. Origin: taphaph, Pronunciation: taw-faf, Definition: 1) to play or sound the timbrel, beat, play upon, drum (on a timbrel or other object)

Pipes: Greek word neqeb Pronunciation: neh'keb, Definition: 1) groove, socket, hole, cavity, settings 1a) technical term relating to jeweler's work

The Sound of Music in Heaven

Now the notes that were coming out of this beautiful being were one note at a time. This being started with a high note and then would go to a low note, then come back to a high note but lower than the previous high note before. Then go back to a low note but higher than the previous low note before. The notes seemed to be layered on top of each other. The high notes on another high note and the lower notes on another lower note. As this being would go from high to low the movement increased between high and low notes. It was moving between each note faster and faster. I had the ability to follow each note as it left the being, no matter how fast they were coming out of the being. I could see the notes coming out of the being's mouth. They had substance to them, but this was a substance that I have not found on earth to compare to, what the notes were made out of. They were on top of each other. You could hold them and walk on them. You could hear and experience each note that came out of this being's mouth.

This beautiful blue being kept singing and producing music until it filled the atmosphere with the sounds of these notes. These notes finally ended up entering the Father on the Throne. I could hear the sounds even as I was leaving Heaven. I could hear the sounds even after I left Heaven. I hear them even now. When this being finally reached the apex or top of praise, it stopped and bowed back on its knees, slowly going down as in an elevator.

What was this beautiful being doing? For a long time after, I would try to sing the music I heard in Heaven. I've tried to hum the sounds and toot the sounds. I tried anything that would produce music to get the sounds out of my head. It was not that the sounds were driving me crazy; I just wanted everyone to hear what I had heard in Heaven.

I would even try to get those who produce music to construct some of the sounds. They all came up way short, because of the boxes or rules that they place music in. I started to realize that I wouldn't be able to get this music out until I came in contact with the "right" person or persons here on earth.

He Hit the Note!

I was in Creswell, Oregon talking to a church about Heaven. The people who had invited us had a little gathering the day before for us to hear a person from Korea who played the violin. As he was playing, he was coming close to some of the sounds I heard in Heaven. They were mostly the sounds I heard from the beautiful light blue being. I asked him if we could find time to see what we could get out of my head in the ways of these sounds. So Sunday after church I sat down with him. He started to play different notes on his violin. As he got closer to the first note that came out of the being's mouth I got excited. Then he hit the note that I first heard come out of the being. I stopped him and said, "That is it! That is it!"

I asked him what note that was. He said the note A.

Then he said in broken English to me that it was amazing that I would recognize that note as the first note that came out of the being's mouth. He proceeded to tell me why he was amazed. He was a concert violinist that played in an orchestra. He said that in an orchestra before they start to play, he and others in the orchestra would tune up off this note A. They would not start to play music until everyone in the orchestra was on the same line as the note A. He was so amazed that I could remember that note above all the others as the first note that came out of the being's mouth.

A Call to Worship

After we discussed this in more detail, I came to understand what this beautiful light blue being was doing. This being was having all the other creations of God tune up off the note of A that was coming from its mouth. It was calling all of Heaven to praise the Father and Jesus, which was this being's purpose.* This being was connecting to all of God's creation to praise God. It connected sounds of substance to each of God's creations in the power of its purpose to bring a sound of praise to God. This being produced notes of praise, in which each note was a full praise for God. Each note connected a heavenly creation to the praise of God the Father.

After the beautiful blue being was back on its knees, I could still hear the sounds that came out of its mouth as the rest of Heaven started to praise God. I saw to the right of me and to the right of the Throne, a large multitude of beings that rose up, as on a number of elevators, off their knees as the first being did. *

The Multitude of Beings

This multitude of beings consisted of heavenly beings and others had been human beings. The numbers were more than I could count. I knew that some of the heavenly beings had been there before the Throne for what seemed to me, to be forever.* Each being was shining and beautiful. The redeemed who had been humans on earth were shining and white as light. The other beings were all colors and shining.*

This multitude started to praise the Father.* Each being was singing a love song to the Father in its own language. I, again, understood all the languages and each song was an individual love song to the Father. Each song sounded so wonderful, so beautiful, so lovely, and so utterly indescribable with human words.* Again, I have tried to hum the sounds, toot the sounds, sing the sounds, and I have not, yet, come close.

When one group of singers was done, another group would rise up, or just one being would rise up. They would rise up off their knees to sing. Again, each note was made with substance. You could hold each note in your hand. Every note was praise in itself. Each being sang out of their innermost being. This kept on happening over and over. These beings were rising up and bowing back down on their knees. They did not sound like they were harmonizing or as a symphony or orchestra would. I saw no instruments. I am not saying that there were no instruments in Heaven. I just did not see any because I was experiencing the sounds coming out of each being. Each being seemed to need no instrument to make the sound of an instrument. Every being's voice has a place in Heaven. I came to understand that God has made a place in Heaven for each of our voices which no one can take away or replace. These voices did not clash with others when praising.

The Crystal-Like Sea's Part in Worship

Now I am about to open an area that few have seen and come back here on earth to tell about. I will not say it was outside of my boxes or thinking. I just did not even think of the things I saw in Heaven as they praised God the Father before His Throne. Again, I just have to tell you what I saw.

After the notes of the multitude of beings left them, the notes seemed to dance as they rose to the Father on the Throne. Before these notes reached the Father, the Crystal-like Sea that was in front of the Throne rose up in the atmosphere and intercepted the notes. Then this sea would make a hole in itself so the notes could dance through.* This seemed to change the sound of the notes, making them higher or lower, like blowing through a horn, flute or some other instrument. It was beautiful! The sounds that came out of the Crystal-like Sea were amazing. The Crystal-like Sea was playing the beings' notes like a person would play the piano. The Crystal-like Sea had been doing this for what seemed to me forever.

Dancing in Heaven

The Crystal-like Sea also made movements in the atmosphere that praised the Father. What wonderful movements of love this Crystal-like Sea performed before the Father. After the notes left the Crystal-like Sea into the atmosphere, the notes met up with the colors coming off the Father.* These colors were alive and would hold onto the notes and dance with them. The colors would dance with the notes all the way back up to the Father and let go, just before the notes would enter the Father.

As I followed the notes passing through the Crystal-like Sea, as it was changing the sounds of the notes and praising the Father with a number of loops in the atmosphere and other movements, I noticed another multitude of beings. This multitude was composed again of some heavenly beings and some were human beings that had been here on earth. These beings were dancing in praise to the Father on the Throne. They were in the atmosphere above the water. These beings were dancing in beautiful motions for the Father on the Throne. Behind the dancing, in front of the dancing, below the dancing, and above the dancing of these beings was the Crystal-like Sea, the colors and the musical notes.

The Thunders of Heaven

The atmospheres were praising the Father on the Throne.* It reminded me of the Fourth of July in the United States of America. We here in the United States would have fire-crackers explode in the atmosphere. The atmospheres in Heaven was popping all over the place in praise for the Father on the Throne. John in Revelation described it as thunder.

REVELATION 14:2 (NKJV)

> "And I heard a voice from heaven, like the voice of many waters, and like the voice of loud thunder. And I heard the sound of harpists playing their harps."

The Beings Flying Around the Father

Then there were the beings flying around the Father on the Throne. There were Living Creatures, as John said in Revelation 4:6-7, 9 ,and seraphim, as Isaiah called them in Isaiah 6:2-4.* These were the beings flying around the Father on the Throne saying, "HOLY, HOLY, HOLY." I saw a multitude of them flying around the Father on the Throne. Some had what looked like eyes on their wings and others did not.* What looked like eyes on the wings would blink, and something would come out of them in praise for the Father on the Throne.

Above the Father on His Throne is His glory, His wonderful glory. Within His glory is His praise for Himself.* Some of you will understand what I just said. Some of you will not. But no one can praise God more than God. For only God knows who He truly is. So His glory only, can praise Him.

This Worship Has Changed My Life

All of what I told you here really falls short of all I saw before the Throne of God. I have not had the questions come my way to tell more, and yet, there is a lot more that takes place before the Throne of God. All I can say is that those of you that know Jesus as Lord and Savior will see all I have tried to disclose to you here and more.

As I saw and listened to this worship before my Father's Throne, I heard a sound so beautiful that it has changed my worship of God forever. This part that I am about to tell you, changed my life the most here on earth. I experienced something about God the Father that changed the way I look at life altogether. It has been hard to explain this to others, typically Christians. When you, as a pure spirit being, get to look at the Father, you see Him completely different than you have seen Him before.

The Father's Love Song

Let me attempt to tell each of you reading this now what I am talking about. I pray that the heart of your understanding is open to receive what I have come to know about our Father God.

Before the Throne, after I saw all that I stated in this chapter, I heard another sound that I had a hard time accepting when I got back to earth. It was a sound that I knew brought life to me, and life more abundantly. This sound was God the Father singing back to each and every being giving Him praise before the Throne.*

He was singing an individual love song to each of His creation. The song was alive and seemed to go inside of the beings it was meant for. What I saw was like what you read in the Song of Solomon in the Bible. Just like in the book Song of Solomon, there is an exchange of love words to each person expressing their love for the other. That is what was going on in Heaven. The Father God was expressing His love for each being and they were expressing their love for Him.

I now believe that happens to us here on earth when we express our love to God. I have not tried to copy His song. What really stirred my spirit was that when the Father sang his song, and it came out of His Spirit, the song was not touched by any other creation. Nothing in Heaven stopped it or would think to stop the song from reaching the targeted being.*

His Love Song for Us Only

With all the songs that came from the heavenly beings to the Father who sits on the Throne, the Crystal-like Sea had its part and the colors had their part in those songs. But when it came to God's song, no one had a part in it but Him and the being it was meant for. This song was pure love. I understood the power of love when I heard this love song that came from the Father.

I knew that not only was the Father sending a love song to each and every creation of His in Heaven, but also on earth. He is sending love to each and every person on the planet. Love from God is being sent out to each and every person all the time, and nothing can stop this love from reaching us.* We can deny His love, reject His love or act like His love is not there, but He keeps sending it to us.* I wish people would really get a hold of what I am writing here. I have stated this before, that every time we take a breath of air, He is saying, "I love you." If you now take a breath of air, listen to the Father telling you that He loves you.

"For God So Loved the World" became more alive to me after seeing and hearing this love song from the Father to each being there. I came to understand that if for some reason, Jesus did not follow through with His part of redeeming us humans on earth, the Father God was going to find another away to reach us and redeem us. He loves us that much!

Chapter 17

God's Creation of Beings

There were several different kinds of beings that I saw in Heaven. There were those who had been humans here on earth and now are among the redeemed in Heaven.* These beings had been on earth and had made Jesus their Lord and Savior while living on this earth.*

Then there were the heavenly creations. They are beings also, but have never known what it is like to be redeemed. I call them beings because they are BEING everything they were created to be. They are perfect in every way, just as the Father, Jesus, and Holy Spirit are perfect.* All I saw was perfect beings. They are RIGHT just like everything around them is RIGHT.* They are the rightness of God because of what Jesus has done for those who had been human here on earth, and for those heavenly beings that never chose to follow Satan.

All of God's beings were being everything that God had created them to be. They were just shining with the glory of the God of all creation. I was experiencing the creation of God as He created it. I experienced life as He created life. I saw life created.*

My Family and Friends Welcome Me

One of the events that, again, blew up one of the boxes that I had believed about Heaven, had to do with families. I had believed that you may recognize your family in Heaven, but I did not really believe it mattered if you did or not. I just looked at it as we were all in the family of God and that is what counted, and that is true. We are all the family of God. But, something happened to me that I did not expect to happen when I was in Heaven.

Jesus was standing to the left of me, and as I said before, He was addressing a half circle of beings. On the other side of Him was my family. I saw my Grandmother Mary, Grandfather Lewis, Grandmother Ruth, Grandfather Begron, and many of my parents' brothers and sisters.* I also saw friends I knew that had died and others I did not know had died. Also, there were a lot of beings that were related to me, but I had never seen them here on earth during my lifetime. I understood they were relatives that had died before I was born. They went back for generations and generations.

At first, I did not know why they were there, but my Grandmother Mary communicated to me why they had all come. She stood out in front of all the others who were my family members and friends. She downloaded into me that they came to welcome me into Heaven. Every family member with whom I was connected because of the DNA inside of me was there; the DNA that God had made me out of.*

There were also past friends that showed up. They had all come to greet me into Heaven. It was going to be a great family reunion if Jesus had not sent me back. To think about it even now, brings me great joy.

My Grandmother Mary

I believe the reason my Grandmother Mary was out in front is because I have always given her credit for praying me into the Kingdom of God. As a child growing up, I can remember going to visit my Grandmother Mary in Houston, Texas. In her house she had a radio on in the kitchen that always had Christian preaching and singing on it. As you went past the kitchen you couldn't help but hear the radio show that was on. I first heard George Foreman preaching on that radio.

This was before he came out with his grills.

So I knew Grandmother had some kind of connection with God. After I accepted Jesus as Lord and Savior at age 17, I told her. She died before I really could talk to her about being born again. Since then it had been in my heart to see my Grandmother Mary when I did get to Heaven, if that were possible. I was just not really sure that would happen. The one person out in front of all the others was her. I was surprised and thrilled.

I have come to believe that those of you that long to see a family member, who has gone on to Heaven before you, will meet this family member right after you meet Jesus. I believe everyone who has made Jesus their Lord and Savior will meet Him first above all else. Your spirit inside of you, the real you, longs to be with your Lord and Savior.

This event changed how I look at my own family that is still here on earth. I did not know if my three brothers or my dad even had a relationship with God. It looked to me as if they did not know Jesus. I knew my mother did because she and I would talk about God every time I called her. We would also pray for each other, so I was sure about her relationship with God. I know that it is up to Jesus and not me to save my family, but when I returned,I wanted to show them the love of God as I had never done before. Because of my belief in Jesus, I had pulled away from my family. I did not have the same interests that they had. So I just did not put a lot of effort into keeping a close relationship with them. When my older brother and dad came through the curtain in the ICU, I remember saying to myself, "I do not know these people." I knew I needed to change that.

Family Matters in Heaven

With that encounter in Heaven with my family members I came to know how important families are to God. I remember experiencing the love they had for me. They still love us even when they are in

Heaven. My family members and friends had pure love for me.* They were glad I was there and they desired for me to be with them. This desire was strong, stronger than the desires we have when praying for our loved ones while we are still living here on earth. This desire that they had for me to be with them is the same desire we have for our loved ones to live with us on earth forever.* People here have asked me if they pray for us there. I said, "No, but they have a great desire for us to be with them there, where everything is right, everything is perfect, and everything is the way God wants it to be."

I understood that these family members do not want to come back here to be on earth.* They are being everything they were created to be. This is not just my family, but every family member of yours that accepted Jesus as Lord and Savior. They are waiting for you to be with them. They are not there praying for you as I said, but again, they have a great desire for you to be there with them, just like Jesus. They have a perfect desire for you to be with them. They really do still love you. I came to understand why we grieve when someone dies. We were never meant to be apart.* That was not in God's plans for us. We die on this earth because of sin and only because of sin.

Bring Back As Many As You Can!

As I stated earlier, my Grandmother Mary looked at me and downloaded a message for the others and for me. She told me to bring as many of us back as I can. I understood that she wanted me to bring as many of our family members back with me as I could. I knew that everyone's family members desired the same thing. They want you that know Jesus as Lord and Savior, to bring as many of your relatives and friends as you can, with you to Heaven.

I came to understand that one of the main reasons Jesus sent me back is to tell you. Jesus has sent us to our own family first. He wants us to talk with them and to pray for them.* I remember telling a person here on earth that it would be a shame if she were the last person in her family to make it to Heaven. It would be a shame. It would be a terrible, terrible shame.

I know that some of you are from families that you would think would never make it to Heaven, but remember that YOU have come out of that family! I know God is doing everything that He possibly can to reach them. He has reached you and is reaching you now, as you read this testimony. Just as my Grandmother Mary said to me, "Bring back as many of your family members with you to Heaven as you can," I believe that all of us should reach as many of our family members as we can. If we that know Jesus as Lord and Savior will reach our own family members, we would reach a lot of people on this planet.

What People Looked Like

My family members in Heaven and others who had been human beings here on earth were shining and had pure joy.* They shine with the glory of God. This shine looked like a long robe but it was really the glory of Jesus coming out of their beings.* That is the only reason they were shining. This brightness was shining out of them and moving as if the wind is blowing it all the time. It was the glory of Jesus and His glory is alive. They had the life of Jesus coming out of them and clothing them in a shining light. This is why there is no darkness. Everything has the glory of God coming out of it. There is no place where darkness can hide. These beings also had a big smile. This was the evidence of the pure joy that they have.

Are Children There?

Heavenly beings do not age because there is no time in Heaven.* People ask me all the time if there are children in Heaven. I tell them that there is no time in Heaven, so there is no aging in Heaven. This does not mean that I did not see what we call children, or young people, or old people. There is just no age in Heaven. They are all beings and they can show you themselves as they want you to see them. They can show themselves as they were when they were young, old, or as a child when they were on earth. So, there are no children in Heaven as we know children here. There is no growing up in Heaven because there is no time. I knew that children below the age of accountability do go to Heaven. So all aborted children are in Heaven, but they are not there as children. They are being everything that God had created them to be. They are beings with pure joy and a big smile.

We Will Still Have Free Will There

Every being had the ability to think in Heaven. They still had the right to choose what they did in Heaven. They just choose the right thing all the time. They all have the ability to move fast. Like I said earlier, all I had to do was think it, and I was there. They all have the ability to have pure love for others. They had more spiritual gifts than you can ever think of here. The only way a person can come close to understanding what they will be like in Heaven is from the Bible. I was a spiritual being that was made in the image of God. I was being what God had made me to be from the beginning of the beginning. I was home and I knew it. You will be home and know it, and you will never leave.

What Will We Be Doing in Heaven?

Since you are in Heaven forever, you are fulfilling your purpose.* I had great joy, and the other beings around me had great joy. They were fulfilling their purpose in Heaven. I have been asked a number of times what we will do there. When I was there, I saw beings doing many things in order to fulfill the desires of God. Some of the beings were before the throne of the Father praising Him. I saw them at every area of praise that I wrote about earlier in this book, singing, dancing, flying, and more. Some beings were in the half circle before Jesus listening to Him as He gave out orders. They had a part to play in the strategy being commanded by Jesus. I have not found the words to tell of everything I saw other beings doing in Heaven, but I knew they all did it with joy. No one was thinking that their purpose was any less than anyone else's purpose.* They all knew that their purpose was important in God's Kingdom.

One of these purposes was to wait on Jesus and the Father, but every creation of God was serving each other.* There was no top or bottom. Every creation was equal.* I saw every creation of God working with the living water, trees, flowers, mountains, valleys, other planets, and what we would call outer space. I saw beings doing something with suns and stars, helping to move them. I saw beings working with the other heavenly beings that we call angels.

Some of the Bible Saints I Saw

I saw Mary who had brought forth Jesus on earth doing something with the living water there in Heaven. What she was doing, I cannot explain to anyone here on earth, because I have not found the words to explain it. I saw Peter and James in the half circle before Jesus. They had a part in the heavenly army of God. I know they were commanders of some type. I saw them move with each command Jesus gave to the unit around them. I knew that Paul was a part of what goes on with praise and worship here on earth. But again, I do not have the English words to say what I knew he was doing. It had something to do with dancing and praising the Lord down here on earth. Abraham had a place that seemed so awesome before the Throne of God. He was taking living light and lifting it up to the Throne of God. God would take it within His hands and toss it in the atmosphere. Now, how do I paint a picture of this for others to understand?

There were more beings doing amazing things of purpose for Jesus and the Father. I just came to understand that we have spiritual gifts that are not added on, but they are us. Our spiritual gifts here on earth are the gifts given to us for the Kingdom of God.

Chapter 18

This Is Not Our Home

2 CORINTHIANS 4:18 (NKJV)

"...while we do not look at the things which are seen, but at the things which are not seen. For the things which are seen are temporary, but the things which are not seen are eternal."

Everything is right and everyone has the right to be in a place of right. Everything there is alive and everyone has a right to live with God forever. I understood that is why we are here; to tell others of who Jesus is so that they can go and be with God.

2 CORINTHIANS 5:1 (NKJV)

"For we know that if our earthly house, this tent, is destroyed, we have a building from God, a house not made with hands, eternal in the heavens."

Everything is alive in Heaven, and no death exists there. God is pure life, light, and love.

We Are Just Passing Through

When I was in Heaven, I knew that I was just passing through down here on earth. It was great to really know that this earth was not my home.* I have always felt that it was not my home, but when I was in Heaven, I knew without a doubt that I was just passing through.

Jesus wants me to make sure that when I tell my story that everyone I talk to knows that the earth is not our home and we who know Jesus as Lord and Savior, are just passing through. Earth is the minority compared to Heaven, where the Father God, Jesus and the Holy Spirit reside. It seemed to me that this earth was just a small part of the big picture, a very small part. But, many people seem to think and act as if this is all that there is.

This Earth is Not Our Home

We are ambassadors here, we who know Jesus as Lord and Savior.* Most of us agree with that, but we do not always act that way here. We act as if this is our home forever, yet Jesus told us that He goes to prepare a place for us. He was not talking about a house as we say many times, but a place in Heaven just for us. When I was there, I knew that I was in my place and no one else could take it. It was prepared for me. I also knew that I was not taking anyone else's place. When I talk about the music there, I understood that each being's song had its own place. I knew I was in my place and no one could take it away. Jesus has a place in Heaven just for you that know Him as Lord and Savior. It was made just for you and no one else.

The earth is not our home. This earth is deteriorating. We are in a countdown to the end of the age. The Bible tells us that. I was reading just the other day about how the temperature has increased on an average of 30% since the 1950s. That means the earth is getting warmer. We have heard from scientists for a while that this is happening. We hear about the rain forest and all the trees being cut down, and what that is doing to this earth. Just the other day, I also read how the Coho Salmon in my area are polluted and that we should not eat so many of them, especially children and pregnant women because they can cause cancer. Then, they went on to talk about other fish in the Puget Sound here in Washington State and how they were polluted and again, we should not eat so many of them.

I could go on about this, but we all are hearing this same information. And yet, we are trying to make this our home, knowing it is not. Today's earth is not as good as yesterday's earth and tomorrow's earth will not be as good as today's.*

My Grandmother Mary wanted me to get this across to other family members here on earth. This was a great desire of hers and the other beings in Heaven. This is a desire of all of God's creation. This is the only desire of our Savior for all of mankind.* God Himself wants us to know that this is not our home and we are only passing through.* We will outlast every problem we have.* We all are going to have to leave this earth someday. We will live on, either in Heaven with God, or in Hell where everything is wrong. But, we are going to have to leave this earth.*

The Elderly Lady

After sharing this story of Heaven in a United Methodist Church in Seattle, Washington, I met an elderly lady who was 91 years old. She had had a stroke a few weeks before we came to share and could not talk or move. She was in a wheelchair when I met her. I looked in her eyes and I knew she believed. Oh, how she believed! I saw faith in her eyes. I have heard people talk about that kind of faith, but I never saw it like that. When I looked in her eyes, it seemed as if they were saying, "Thank you, thank you and thank you." Then, they seemed to change a little, and it seemed to me she was saying, "Will you come and visit me?" I said to her, "I will come and see you." She then pulled me down to where my ear was close to her mouth, and she asked, "When?" The pastor had told me that she could not talk or move. When she pulled me down, and said, "When?" it was the first word she had spoken since having the stroke. That was a glorious time to experience that. I did go see her a few weeks later in a nursing home and she was moving and talking even more.

When I died, I knew where to go and no one was telling me where to go. I was like a salmon going home. No one had to tell me. And when I got there, I knew I was supposed to be in my place. Everything was right, and I was right where I was supposed to be. I was home. I was home. I was home. I WAS HOME! *

Chapter 19

Angels

> "Angel" is a word often used to describe a supernatural appearance of a heavenly being. (Luke 24:34, Acts 2:3; 7:2,30,35; 9:17; 13:31; 16:9; 26:16).

As I have told this story, I have had a lot of questions about angels asked of me. I have not focused on angels for one reason. We as humans like to make gods out of God creations, and angels are one of them.* Humans also like to make gods out of evil spirits, devils, and demons.* We need to understand that angels are one of God's creations, and we are not to worship them in anyway. They are made for His purpose.* They are not to be worshipped. Only God the Father, Son, and Holy Spirit are to be worshipped. Only God!

People would probably see more angels, but angels do not want to be seen or to be worshipped. I came to really understand this because of what happened to me. Worship and praise was only made for God. To understand what I am going to write about angels, you must first understand the meaning of the word "angels".

> **Hebrew Meaning:** mal'ak Kalm 1a) messenger, representative; 1b) messenger; 1c) angel; 1d) the theophanic angel From an unused root meaning to dispatch as a deputy; a messenger; specifically, of God, i.e. an angel (also a prophet, priest or teacher):-ambassador, angel, king, messenger.

> **Greek Meaning:** aggelos aggelov: a messenger, envoy, one who is sent, an angel, a messenger from God. From aggello (to bring tidings); a messenger; especially an "angel"; by implication, a pastor:-angel, messenger.

The name does not denote their nature, but their office as messengers. In Heaven there are no angels, they are looked at as a loving creation of God. They are only an angel when they are being sent as a messenger from God to others. Now that you have these meanings let us look at these verses to understand that angels come in every size and shape. Some look like humans and some do not.*

REVELATION 4:6-9 (NKJV)

> "Before the throne there was a sea of glass, like crystal. And in the midst of the throne, and around the throne, were four living creatures full of eyes in front and in back. The first living creature was like a lion, the second living creature like a calf, the third living creature had a face like a man, and the fourth living creature was like a flying eagle. The four living creatures, each having six wings, were full of eyes around and within. And they do not rest day or night, saying: "Holy, Holy, Holy, Lord God Almighty, Who was and is and is to come!" Whenever the living creatures give glory and honor and thanks to Him who sits on the throne, who lives forever and ever."

I saw these creations of God at work in Heaven. There are a lot of activities here on earth in which the angels are working at the command of God. They are part of a massive army fighting for the souls of humans. Every one of them has a purpose and is very happy in completing their purpose. They also have great joy and smile a lot.

The Horse-Like Angels

The first angels that I really did notice were what we would call horses. There were so many horses. It was surprising to me.* And yet when you read the Bible you see in Revelation where Jesus is coming back on a white horse.* There is also a red, a black, and a pale horse mentioned.*

Now not every horse looks like what we think horses should look like. Some have the head of a horse and the body of a human. Some have a head of a human and the body of a walking upright horse. Each horse-like being has a purpose. Some were at the Throne, and others were with Jesus when He was addressing the other beings. But they were all moving according to the will of God by choice. All the angels still have a choice to serve God.

Some of these horse beings had wings. Some had wings like that of a shark fin, and others had two or more wings like that of birds, bats, and helicopters. Yes, it was different than what I thought it would be. These horses were moving all over the place and were moving very fast.

Many of the beings that I saw in Heaven, people would call animals, but they are not like the animals we have here on earth. In Heaven they are simply beings made by God.

The Little Angels

There are very little angels that reminded me of fairies. They are not fairies, but they are angels or heavenly beings. One person asked me if the little angels have just as much power as the bigger angels do, and the answer is yes. The smaller angels have just as much power as the bigger angels do because they are working under the authority of God. It is God that gives them power.* We think of power as big. It has everything to do with God's love. God's entire Kingdom moves in the power of God's love and this is REAL power. When we understand who really has the power and what that power is, we will overcome a number of things that get in the way of God's love expressed to us.

The Bull-Like Angel

Now another angel that I saw resembled a bull. The bull-like being was big, about seven feet tall. He was shiny just like all the other beings there. This bull-like being had the body of a human with hands, but the feet were like that of a bull. He looked mean to me at first. I saw a ring coming out of his nose and the ring was alive. But, when I looked in his eyes, I saw love, pure love. He loved all of God's creation that is right. His purpose was to fight for righteousness. In any battle that takes place for righteousness, this being is there, fighting in the spiritual dimension. There was more than one of these bull-like creations.

The Angels Are Fulfilling God's Purpose

God has many angels that do the same for hope, salvation, faith, and healing as the bull-like creation does for righteousness. You see, our battle is first in the heavenlies, and then it is transferred down here on earth.

EPHESIANS 6:12 (NKJV)

> "For we do not wrestle against flesh and blood, but against principalities, against powers, against the rulers of the darkness of this age, against spiritual hosts of wickedness in the heavenly places."

All of God's creation is beautiful in His purpose. Purpose combined with God's love makes all of God's creations beautiful. So, what do angels look like? Well, they could and do look like every creation that is here on earth and more. Anything here on earth that is alive could be looked at as an angel in Heaven. They are all doing what God created them to do with love. They are messengers of love to us from God.

I know this is hard for us to hear because many of us look at angels as gods here on earth, instead of as an extension of God's Love to others. The angels of God know this and act in this way.

They do all they do within the love of God. In the will of God is beauty, so all you need to know, is that.

Do We Have Guardian Angels?

One of the most asked questions I get is, "Do we have Guardian Angels?" The answer is yes.* They do what God has ordered them to do for us. They follow His will. We have more than one.* How many does each person that knows Jesus as Lord and Savior have? The number of angels we have is based on whether or not we are fulfilling our purpose here on earth. They are all doing what they are created to do for God in Heaven with love.* There are no weak angels, as I stated earlier. Their power and strength has to do with God's purpose for them.

This spiritual war that is going on is bigger than most of us want to believe. When you trust our Father for a breakthrough in your life or someone else's life, a lot happens in the spiritual dimension that you may not even be aware of. For everyone that has come to know Jesus as Lord and Savior, there was a great battle that took place in the spiritual dimension for your soul. Since the fall of Lucifer, many angels have taken their place in the battle. Again, they are messengers of love to us from God.

What Do Angels Look Like?

Maybe one out of four angels that I saw in Heaven looked human.* There are angels that look like human men and women, but their gender does not affect their purpose. Angels are genderless; they only look like male or female.* There are angels that look like light, fire, water, air, clouds, wind, trees, and flowers.* I could go on, but really understand this one thing; they are all beautiful because they are doing God's will, and in the will of God is beauty. That is the most important thing to remember.

So for now, know that there are more angels that stayed with God than went with Satan.* Someday I will teach on this area about angels more, when I think it will not lead to more angel worship. I end this chapter with this. We are only to worship God the Father, Son, and Holy Spirit, not angels. *

Chapter 20

Eight Things I Was Told About the End of the Age

When I was in Heaven with Jesus and the Father, Jesus communicated these eight things to me that would signal the end of the age. They were not given to me in a certain order. Some are happening right now, others are beginning to happen, and others are still to come. The one I really like is the one that tells of prayer increasing and spiritual eyes opening. We need to be in more prayer for us to see what God sees.

These Eight Things Will Take Place To Signal the End of the Age!

(They are not in any order.)

- EVERY NATION IS HERE FOR THE PURPOSE OF GOD!*
- KINGS AND QUEENS, OR WHAT YOU CALL PRESIDENTS AND PRIME MINISTERS, ARE ALL PUT IN POWER FOR THE PURPOSE OF GOD! *
- MORE EVERYDAY SONS AND DAUGHTERS OF GOD WILL BE PLACED IN RULERSHIP OF NATIONS FOR THE PURPOSE OF GOD!*

- RAISING PEOPLE FROM THE DEAD WILL BE COMMON IN THE LAST DAYS OF THE AGE!*

- GOD IS NOT WORKING THROUGH ONE PERSON, BUT THROUGH HIS SONS AND DAUGHTERS IN THE PRESENT AGE. STOP PEOPLE FROM CHASING MEN AND HAVE THEM FOLLOW GOD!*

- THE GOOD NEWS OF GOD IS NOT FOR SALE AND HE IS GOING TO STOP THE SELLING OF IT BY HAVING MORE PEOPLE GIVE WHAT THEY KNOW AWAY.

- FREELY IT HAS BEEN GIVEN AND FREELY THEY MUST GIVE! *

- THAT WHICH IS EVIL WILL LOOK GOOD, EVEN TO THE SONS AND DAUGHTERS OF GOD. THE SONS AND DAUGHTERS OF GOD WILL GROW IN PRAYER IN THAT TIME AND NEW EYES WILL OPEN—SPIRITUAL EYES. THEY WILL SEE FROM THE HEART! *

- VISUAL DECEPTION WILL INCREASE IN ALL AREAS OF THE WORLD! *

Chapter 21

What Was I in Heaven?

What was it like to be in heaven as a being? You are being who God truly made you to be. You lack nothing. In Heaven you are a part of everything and everything is a part of you. You experience everything there, all at once. All at one time, your current spiritual gifts explode and keep intensifying. It is like jumping into cold water and having all of your senses activated at the same time. Imagine smelling, tasting, seeing, feeling, and hearing the water all at the same time. That is how it is in Heaven when it comes to your spiritual gifts.

Our Spiritual Gifts and Abilities

In Heaven spiritual gifts are added to the ones you have here on earth. No drug here on earth can compare with what you will experience there. There, everything is made to be a part of you. When you see something, you experience it with no imperfection.

We do not always use our spiritual gifts here in a consistent way. We have the ability to use them all the time, but in the fight with our carnal self, we more often than not end up not using what we have. We just do not use them as often as we should, here on earth. But there, we have more spiritual gifts than here. There are more new spiritual gifts that come alive when you are in Heaven. I just do not have anything here on earth to compare with these other spiritual gifts. There are spiritual gifts in Heaven that you have never experienced here on earth.

How I Traveled in Heaven

Just as we have new spiritual gifts in Heaven, we have new abilities to do things in Heaven that we cannot do in this body. Since coming back, I have come to understand more about my body and what it can and cannot do. In Heaven, my spirit has no limits; not like my body here on earth. You move fast. When I left this body, I was at Jesus's feet faster than a person can blink. When I wanted to move, I just thought of being somewhere else and I was there.

I could pass through anything and everything, not that you always did because of respect for other beings. I would always ask for permission. When you enter a room you could go through what we call walls. But again remember, everything is alive, even the buildings. The buildings have doors and gates, but I did not have to use them. Now, I would out of respect for the buildings, because they were alive. Everything is alive, so I would ask. I was at the top of mountains, bottom of seas or water, in trees, under bushes, on dirt or ground, walking through grass and flowers. I did all of this just by thinking about it. I would fly, or what we would call flying. It was more like just being a part of this living atmosphere: golden, white, and alive. What an atmosphere!

What more can I write? It is hard to explain to others what "everything is right" feels like. It is not a feeling but an experience. It is hard for others to understand with their mind what it is like where the Father and Jesus are. That is something you will only understand when you come to know who you really are—a created spirit of God. Because we are spirit, soul, and body, we have to let our spirit become alive in God's Kingdom. We have the ability to choose whom we serve; whether it is God or ourselves.

What did I look like? I was shining because of the Father and Jesus. They shone out of me.

Chapter 22

Who Am I Now After Heaven?

After I left the hospital knowing that I had been to Heaven and back, I did not want to misuse this gift that I had experienced. I prayed to God and asked Him to help me not be tempted to make a lot of money off of this experience. Even if I had great riches here on earth, what would they be compared to what I have in Heaven? Not a thing. When you have Jesus, you have everything you need.

So the Father God and I came up with two things for me to follow to stay away from pride.

One of those things is to have my wife speak before me when she is able to be with me and to allow her as much time as she needs to tell her side of the story. I have been in places where they have given us an hour to speak and she has taken 45 minutes to tell her side of the story. That left me with only 15 minutes. Most of the time people have asked me to keep going or have asked us back. But my wife, when she speaks, can take as much time as she wants to tell what she knows.

I have always felt that I have a special message for each and every person I have come back to talk to. Numbers are not a big thing to me. God knows who He sent me back to. I just have to go and tell them. I have presented to thousands of people at a time, and then, on the other hand, to just one person at a time. I have had the honor to speak to one complete family, from great grandparents to great, great grandchildren. Whoever I speak to and the number of people I speak to does not matter to me as long as I speak to whomever God wants me to speak to. All I have to do is do what He wants me to do.

I Only Talk About What People Ask Me

The other area that God and I came up with to keep me from pride is that I would not talk about anything that I have not been asked a question about. All that I have written in this book is based on questions that people have asked me about the experience. I would have question and answer sessions so that people would ask me as many questions as possible. I have been in some question and answer meetings that lasted up to six hours. There are still many questions that have not been asked.

Before going to Heaven and coming back, I would stay away from anything that had to do with people asking me questions about the Bible. I knew why I believed in what I believed, but I did not want to answer questions on things I did not know about or even things I did know about. I did not want to get into any arguments over anything when it came to the Bible.

The other reason I did not like to answer questions is because I did not want others to know that I did not know something (being a minister). But now, I am ready to take on any question given me. If I do not know, that is OK. I say to people many times that I only need to know what God wants me to know. Most people I say that to, do not understand what I am saying. But when I was in Heaven, there was no wasting of anything. So I try not to use my thinking on things that are not important.

Four Main Areas of Questions

The first area of questions usually comes from children. A child's most asked question is, "Is it going to be fun in heaven?" Children ask some of the best questions. They usually ask the most questions that are "out of the box". Much of what I tell people comes from their questions. They just seem to have this way of thinking that they know they are going to Heaven; they just want to know how much fun they are going to have.

The second area of questions is from teenagers who want to know more about their belief system. Their questions are designed to get more information to help them establish a belief system.

They want to know more about this God. Is He really real? They also have a way of asking questions "outside of the box".

The third area of questions is from some adults. Their questions are questions that are posed to support their beliefs. They want to find out if God fits in the box they've created for Him. Sometimes I support what someone had believed before. Sometimes I expand on what someone had believed about God. And sometimes I give them information that just blows up the box they built for God. I tell them many times that He did not fit in the box that I had created for Him. As you have read, many of these boxes were blown up that I had put God in.

The fourth and last area of questions is from the elderly. Their questions are similar to those questions that children ask. They are coming to the reality that they are close to going home, and just want to know how it is going to be.

My Number One Job

I ask everyone who reads this to understand that I have a job to do down here on earth, and until it is done I cannot go back home. What is that job? My job is to bring as many people with me to Heaven as I can. This is no different than for anyone else who has accepted Jesus as their Lord and Savior.

When I was in Heaven I had pure joy. I know that everyone who comes before Jesus as a son of God will have pure joy. Anyone who Jesus can see Himself in, that person will have pure joy. I also know that those that come before Jesus that do not know Him as Lord and Savior will experience pure terror. The greatest pain a person who has not accepted Jesus as Lord and Savior will experience is the separation from Jesus and the Father God forever.

I know that I am not a part of this world as I felt before. Even when I knew I was going to be with God someday, I still felt like this was home for now. Now after my experience, I do not feel like this is my home at all. My home is with God, my Father. I even call the time that I take to pray, going home. For me, praying is like going home for a time. I sometimes just want to pray all day for I feel so at home while I am praying. Even just writing this down for you to read brings me to the point of wanting to stop and pray. I know He hears our prayers. Yes, we that know Jesus as Lord and Savior, He hears our prayers from our heart, not from our head.

It's Taken Some Time to Re-Adjust

There are times when I feel very out of place here on earth. I can retreat inward for long periods of time. I feel as if I never left there. I will be glad when all this mess on earth is over and every part of God's creation is right. It seems to me that I am in between two dimensions, the real and the not-real. For most people, the earth is the real dimension and Heaven is not. For me, it is the other way around. I see this world falling apart every day. I know that today is better than tomorrow and yesterday was better than today. I do not mean in my spirit and God's kingdom, I am actually talking about the physical world we live on. The ground, trees, plants, water, and everything we can see, hear, and touch are falling apart because of the curse that was brought on us by Adam, man. I see the evidence of this decay every day. This is good and bad. In me, I cry to see many more souls saved, and at the same time, I feel and see how short the time is that we have before I could return to Heaven. So what is the real dimension?

I think a lot slower now when answering others. I do not like to waste words. We say a lot of things here on earth that is just the answer we are used to giving. Here is an example: "How are you doing?" Most people say, "Good" or "OK", or something that we have been programmed to answer with. Now, I have to make sure that I am the words I say, because there, in Heaven, you waste no words. Communication was all right, so you did not say a lot, but what you did say was truth.

Now again, you did not communicate with words out loud that much. You could if you wanted to, but mostly every being just gave you what they were thinking. Sometimes I ask my wife or son something in my head and then, believe I have said it out loud. They have now helped me to remember to talk out loud. Sometimes I have to remind myself to talk out loud too. I do not have the need to pray out loud so others can hear me. I know My Father hears me loud and clear whether I say it out loud or not. It must come from my heart. I know He hears me and will answer my prayer.

Praying for the sick, that have Jesus as their Lord and Savior, was hard. I knew that if they died they would go to Heaven to be with my Father, their Father. But, God let me know, that until their purpose is done on earth I am to always pray for healing. God is the only one who knows when a child of God's time is up. It is also hard for me to receive any praise for what I do or say now. When I was with the Father and Jesus in Heaven, only the Father and Jesus received praise.

I now understand this last idea more than I ever had before. "Relationship" is the only thing that will last. We can take a relationship we have with another child of God with us to Heaven.

When people come to know Jesus as Lord and Savior through how I am serving my Father, then I will have a relationship with them forever. And it will be all right. Yes!

You Did This For Me

From the beginning of time
From the Old testament to the New
Stories were written of a place
Where there were no worries or cares
There are streets of gold
Musical notes springing from waterfalls of crystal
Lights that shine brighter than the sun
On the hottest summer day
Every color imaginable shine
From the crystal edges of His crown
His robe of the purest white
Draped over His golden brass colored feet
Songs of praise and worship to the Father filled the open sky
As the spirits danced thankful for favor, grace and mercy
Kneeling down at the feet of our brother Jesus Christ
A light beamed from the palms of both His hands
Uttered from my lips these five words:
You did this for me!

By Dorothea Elisha Holmes

Chapter 23

Last Comments

Over the past 33 years I have worked with people in the social field, mostly with teenagers and their families. I worked in King County Superior Court employed as a Juvenile Drug Court/Chemical Dependency Disposition Alternative Program Manager. I have also worked as a Program/Project Manager for King County's Mental Health, Chemical Abuse and Dependency Service Division. I was employed in the U.S. Air Force on active duty for six years and in the Air Force Reserve for another 14 years, with 18 of those years as a Chemical Dependency Counselor and Human Relations and Equal Opportunity Counselor. In the past, I have been a Director for an inpatient treatment/transitional-housing program, a Substance Abuse Prevention Coordinator for King County, and a Chemical Dependency Coordinator for two outpatient youth treatment programs. I have helped train over 400 parents in parenting skills and given over 1000 trainings and presentations dealing with subjects addressing human service issues. I have coordinated prevention, treatment, family conferences, and have been on television and radio discussing subjects concerning human services issues. I helped develop a number of model programs that have been funded by the U.S. government, King County and private industries. I have been on many committees representing Washington State, King County, and many cities.

About two years ago I left this work to tell this story to as many people as possible. I have done it across the United States and in other countries. But what is on my heart is to reach the young people all around the world. In my heart are many young people who have not really had an encounter with the all-powerful God.

In the coming years I am praying that I can make this heavenly experience a reality to the youth of this world. I hope to do this through a number of ways: Comics, Videos, Video/Board Games, clothing, music, and many more books. Somehow, we must reach that generation that we believe are lost.

I do not want Jesus to come back soon, because there are still so many to tell about Him. I was where He is and He truly wants everyone in Heaven. I heard the sounds from Hell. If you heard them, you truly would not even want any of your enemies to go there. That is not the will of God. So, in these last days that I am on this earth, I want to reach those kids. Pray that I do and can.

The Restoring Children International supports many in Peru. Dean Braxton Ministries strongly supports the girls' home named "La Familia Internacional" (The Inernational Family) in Arequipa. This home gives shelter and care, around the clock, to girls ranging from 3-20 years of age. These girls come from juvenile court institutions (what we would call foster care) and even sometimes they are left by parents and grandparents who are unable to care for them. For more information about Restoring Children International Ministries go to www.restoring children.org, write to PO Box 2128, Leavenworth, WA 98826 or Call Rick Daviscourt at 509.845.4929.

Again, we must in these last days, reach as many as we can in our own countries and around the world. We must reach as many as we can before they go to Hell and not Heaven. Both of these are very real places. We do have a choice to make.

What are You Going to Do With This Information?

I have done my best to share my experience in this book. I hope this has helped you to really choose who you want to serve in your last days here on earth. I want you to experience all that I did and more. Yes, there is a lot more to Heaven that I did not speak about or even experience myself. You see, what we call Heaven, is ever-expanding. God is still creating. Nothing dies there. Yes, there is a lot more waiting for you there. I want you to see all of God's living creation.

Right now, make Jesus the Savior of your soul and spirit, which is the real you. Ask God to become Lord of your life. Do it in your own words, or say these: "Jesus, I ask you to forgive me of all I have done wrong, those actions I remember and those I do not remember. I want you to be my Savior and Lord now. Thank you for making a way so that I can live with you forever and ever. I ask this in my Savior Jesus's name. Amen."

For some of you this may not fit because you have said it before without real meaning. Well now, make a new commitment to him. Ask Him to forgive you for not following through before and to help you follow through this time. Say it in your own words. Say it from your heart.

Now if you have made that commitment to follow the Lord Jesus, you too will know what it is like to say, "You Did This For Me, Thank You, Thank You, Thank You!"

I Realized My Home is Yet to Come

I walked into the sanctuary
Not knowing what to expect
All I knew was
I was tired, bone deep
I sat down in the front pew
Hoping to hear
Hear something
I just needed something
A man came to the podium to speak
He had a kind face
An honest face
So rare
He started talking of a place
It was a place I knew of
But had never been made real
A place called heaven
When he talked
I became entranced
I could see the water
I could see the color
He was describing my childhood memories
The fields I had run
The trees I had climbed
The ocean I had played in
The safety I felt in my parent's home
The love I had felt
The songs they sang over me
Knowing they were watching over me
The completeness, wholeness
I longed for those days again
To feel so carefree
To know you were always loved

To never know fear
But that was not my childhood
That was what was to come
I almost wanted to cry
How did I have memories,
Of a place I had never been?
Why did I feel Like he just described
my childhood home?
The congregation stands up to go home
But my home wasn't home anymore
I realized
my home is yet to come.

By Teresa Smith

Chapter Notes

I have listed the scripture references by whole passages in hopes that you would study them in their entire settings to fully understand these verses. You will find that some key scriptures relating to my testimony will be fully printed out or shortened within parenthesis.

Chapter 1 Notes

"No, It Is Not Your Time"

Subtitle: None

Line: What I do remember, is the first time I was before Jesus He said, "No, It is not your time. Go back."

> Luke 12: 16-21, v.20 "But God said to him, 'Fool! This night your soul will be required of you; then whose will those things be which you have provided?'"
>
> Eccl. 9:12, Job 22:15-16 (verse 16)

Line: At the edge of heaven is thick darkness—a blackness such as you will never experience here on earth.

Rev 16:10-11, v.10 "Then the fifth angel poured out his bowl on the throne of the beast, and his kingdom became full of darkness; and they gnawed their tongues because of the pain."

Ex 10:21-23 (verse 22), Mat 8:12, Mat 22:13, Mat 25:30

Line: This second time I reached the edge of Heaven, I heard the cries of those who were in Hell.

Rev 20:13 "...and Death and Hades (Hell) delivered up the dead who were in them."

Job 26:6, Luke 8:26-31 (verse 31)

Subtitle: A Simple Operation

Line: I know EVERYTHING IS RIGHT, where Jesus is, and THERE IS NOTHING WRONG!

Ps 119:142 "Your righteousness is an everlasting righteousness,"

Luke 12:32-34 (verse 33), John 8:31-36 (verses 32,36), 2 Cor 5:20-21 (verse 21), Phil 3:8-11 (verse 9)

Line: Some say it is peaceful, but it far exceeds peace because there is nothing to be peaceful from.

Phil 4:6-9, v. 7 "and the peace of God, which surpasses all understanding, will guard your hearts and minds through Christ Jesus."

v. 9 "The things which you learned and received and heard and saw in me, these do, and the God of peace will be with you."

John 14:25-28 (verse 27), Eph 2:14-18 (verses 14,17)

Line: Some say it is peaceful, but it far exceeds peace because there is nothing to be peaceful from.

Rev 21:22-27, v.27 "But there shall by no means enter it anything that defiles, or causes an abomination or a lie, but only those who are written in the Lamb's Book of Life."

Line: When I first arrived in Heaven and knelt before Jesus, all I could do was say, "YOU DID THIS FOR ME?!! THANK YOU, THANK YOU, THANK YOU, THANK YOU, THANK YOU, and THANK YOU!!"

Ps 79:13 "...will give You thanks forever; We will show forth Your praise to all generations."

Ps 34:1-3, Ps 63:2-6 (verses 3-5), Ps 118:19-21 (verses 19,21)

Chapter 2 Notes

I Am Just a Man

Subtitle: None

Line: I must let everyone know I was sent back to do the same thing that all of us that accept Jesus into our lives as Lord and Savior are supposed to do.

Mat 28:16-20, v.19 "Go therefore and make disciples of all the nations, baptizing them in the name of the Father and of the Son and of the Holy Spirit,"

v. 20 "teaching them to observe all things that I have commanded you; and lo, I am with you always, even to the end of the age." Amen.

Mark 16:14-18 (verses 15-18), Luke 24:46-53 (verses 4748), Acts 1:7-8 (verse 8)

Subtitle: What Really Matters Is That You Are There!

Line: What will matter is that you are there!

> Heb 11:15-16, v. 16" But now they desire a better, that is, a heavenly country. Therefore God is not ashamed to be called their God, for He has prepared a city for them."
>
> John 14:1-6 (verse 6), 2Cor 4:14

Line: I do not have to perform to get in Heaven, and you do not have to perform either.

> Gal 1:10 "For if I still pleased men, I would not be a bondservant of Christ."
>
> John 9:4

Line: There are many people in Heaven whom I did not think would make it but did, and many whom I believed would make it but did not. Jesus knows the heart of a person.

> Mat 7:21-23, v. 21 "Not everyone who says to Me, 'Lord, Lord,' shall enter the kingdom of heaven, but he who does the will of My Father in heaven."
>
> > v. 23 "And then I will declare to them, 'I never knew you; depart from Me, you who practice lawlessness!'"
>
> Mat 22:11-13 (verse 13), Rom 11:19-22 (verses 20-21)

Line: All I can say is that when He looked at me, He saw Himself, and I was accepted into Heaven.

> Gal 2:17-20, v.20 "I have been crucified with Christ; it is no longer I who live, but Christ lives in me; and the life which I now live in the flesh I live by faith in the Son of God, who loved me and gave Himself for me."
>
> Eph 3:14-19 (verses 16-17), Col 1:27-29 (verse 27)

Chapter 3 Notes

Everything Is Right "You Did This For Me?!!"

Subtitle: Thank You, Thank You, Thank You....

Line: Again, I repeat that I know everything is RIGHT where Jesus is and there is nothing wrong.

> John 8:31-36, v.32"And you shall know the truth, and the truth shall make you free."
>
> v. 36 "Therefore if the Son makes you free, you shall be free indeed".
>
> Luke 12:32-34 (verse 33), Rev 21:6-7 (verse 7)

Line: Some say it is peaceful, but it far exceeds peace because there is nothing to be peaceful from in Heaven.

> Rev 21:22-27, v. 27 " But there shall by no means enter it anything that defiles, or causes an abomination or a lie, but only those who are written in the Lamb's Book of Life."

Line: When I first stood before Jesus, all I could do was say, "YOU DID THIS FOR ME?!!, THANK YOU, THANK YOU, THANK YOU, THANK YOU, THANK YOU, THANK YOU!"

> Ps 138:1-5, v. 1 "I will praise You with my whole heart; Before the gods I will sing praises to You."
>
> v. 2 "I will worship toward Your holy temple, And praise Your name For Your loving-kindness and Your truth; For You have magnified Your word above all Your name"
>
> v. 4 "All the kings of the earth shall praise You, O LORD, when they hear the words of Your mouth"
>
> v. 5 "Yes, they shall sing of the ways of the LORD, for great is the glory of the LORD."

Ps 34:1-3, Ps 63:2-5 (verses 3-5), Ps 79:13, Ps 118:19-21 (verse 19)

Line: When I first got there, all I wanted to do or could do was praise Jesus.

Ps 103:1-5, v.1 "Bless the LORD, O my soul; And all that is within me, bless His holy name!"

v.2 "Bless the LORD, O my soul, And forget not all His benefits:"

Ps 118:15-18 (verse 17), Luke 19:37-40 (verses 37-38)

Line: No one had to tell me. I just knew what to do. I knew that we praise Jesus and Father God, no one else.

John 4:23-24, v.23" But the hour is coming, and now is, when the true worshipers will worship the Father in spirit and truth; for the Father is seeking such to worship Him."

v. 24 "God is Spirit, and those who worship Him must worship in spirit and truth."

Mat 21:15-16 (verse 16), Phil 3:17-21 (verses 20-21)

Line: The only ones who receive praise are the Father and Jesus in Heaven, they are THE ONLY ONES.

1 Cor 1:27-31, v.29 "that no flesh should glory in His presence."

v.31 "that, as it is written, "He who glories, let him glory in the LORD."

Isa 2:11-12 (verse 11), Rev 21:22-27 (verses 22-23)

Subtitle: Praising Him Was All I Needed

Line: Everything within me praised Him. Everything I was made of cried out in praise to Jesus.

> Ps 103:1-5, v.1" Bless the LORD, O my soul; And all that is within me, bless His holy name! "
>
> > v.2 "Bless the LORD, O my soul, And forget not all His benefits"
> >
> > Ps 118:15-18 (verse 17), Luke 19:37-40 (verses 37-38)

Line: Not my body, of course, since it stayed here on earth, but my spirit and soul—the real me, worshipped with my whole being.

> 1 Cor 15:50-54, v.50" Now this I say, brethren, that flesh and blood cannot inherit the kingdom of God; nor does corruption inherit incorruption."
>
> > v.53" For this corruptible must put on incorruption, and this mortal must put on immortality."
> >
> > v.54 "So when this corruptible has put on incorruption, and this mortal has put on immortality, then shall be brought to pass the saying that is written: "Death is swallowed up in victory."
>
> 2 Cor 5:1-10 (verses 1-2,4,6,8), Ps 103:14-17 (verse 14)

Line: Not my body, of course, since it stayed here on earth, but my spirit and soul—the real me, worshipped with my whole being.

> John 4:21-24, v.23 "But the hour is coming, and now is, when the true worshipers will worship the Father in spirit and truth; for the Father is seeking such to worship Him."
>
> > v.24 "God is Spirit, and those who worship Him must worship in spirit and truth."
>
> Ps 119:171-175 (verse 175), Ps 94:16-19 (verse 17)

Line: During the praising it seem like I was turning into God's LOVE.

> 1 John 4:16-17, v.16" And we have known and believed the love that God has for us. God is love, and he who abides in love abides in God, and God in him"
>
> > v. 17" Love has been perfected among us in this: that we may have boldness in the day of judgment; because as He is, so are we in this world."
>
> Cor 13:4-8, Eph 5:1-2 (verse 2)

Line: I felt pure JOY. It seemed to me that I could live off the praising.

> Luke 10:17-20, v.17 "Then the seventy returned with joy, saying, "Lord, even the demons are subject to us in Your name."
>
> > v.20 "Nevertheless do not rejoice in this, that the spirits are subject to you, but rather rejoice because your names are written in Heaven."
>
> Ps. 4:6-8 (verse 7), Eccl 2:24-26 (verse 26), Isa 12:2-3 (verse 3), Rom 15:13

Line: I did not need any food. Praising Him seemed to be all I needed.

> John 4:31-34, v.34" Jesus said to them, 'My food is to do the will of Him who sent Me, and to finish His work.'"
>
> Lam 3:20-26 (verses 22-23)

Line: Not because of what I did, but what He did for me when I accepted Him as my Lord and Savior.

> 2 Tim 1:8-10, v.9 "who has saved us and called us with a holy calling, not according to our works, but according to His own purpose and grace which was given to us in Christ Jesus before time began"
>
> Rom 15:17-19 (verse 18), Titus 3:3-9 (verses 5,7-8)

Subtitle: I Saw Jesus On the Cross

Line: I knew what He did on the cross was for me.

Rom 10:9-13, v.13 "For whoever calls on the name of the LORD shall be saved."

Eph 1:3-14 (verse 6), Tit 2:11-12 (verse 11)

Line: I knew that, I knew.

1 Cor 13:12-13, v.12 "For now we see in a mirror, dimly, but then face to face. Now I know in part, but then I shall know just as I also am known"

Heb 12:22-24

Line: The only reason I was in Heaven with Him was because of what He had done for me, and I knew it. I knew I was complete or perfect because of what He had done.

John 3:13-18, v.14 "And as Moses lifted up the serpent in the wilderness, even so must the Son of Man be lifted up"

v. 15 "that whoever believes in Him should not perish but have eternal life."

v.16 "For God so loved the world that He gave His only begotten Son, that whoever believes in Him should not perish but have everlasting life"

v. 17 "For God did not send His Son into the world to condemn the world, but that the world through Him might be saved"

v. 18 "He who believes in Him is not condemned; but he who does not believe is condemned already, because he has not believed in the name of the only begotten Son of God"

Is 53:4-5, John 1:29-31 (verse 29)

Line: The only reason I was in Heaven with Him was because of what He had done for me, and I knew it. I knew I was complete or perfect because of what He had done.

> 2 Cor 5:16-21, v.17 "Therefore, if anyone is in Christ, he is a new creation; old things have passed away; behold, all things have become new"
>
> > v. 19 "that is, that God was in Christ reconciling the world to Himself, not imputing their trespasses to them, and has committed to us the word of reconciliation"
> >
> > v. 21 "For He made Him who knew no sin to be sin for us, that we might become the righteousness of God in Him"
>
> Rom 6:1-4 (verse 4), Col 4:12

Line: I knew He saw Himself in me and I was allowed into Heaven.

> 1 John 5:9-12, v.11 "And this is the testimony: that God has given us eternal life, and this life is in His Son"
>
> > v. 12 "He who has the Son has life; he who does not have the Son of God does not have life"
>
> Luke 12:8-9 (verse 8), 1 John 4:13-16 (verses 13,16)

Line: It was all of His works. Even the good works I had done was Him working through me.

> Col 3:14-24, v.17 "And whatever you do in word or deed, do all in the name of the Lord Jesus, giving thanks to God the Father through Him"
>
> > v. 23 "And whatever you do, do it heartily, as to the Lord and not to men, 24 knowing that from the Lord you will receive the reward of the inheritance; for you serve the Lord Christ."
>
> Ps. 44:1-3 (verse 3), Phil 2:13-14 (verse 13)

Line: I knew it was for others also, but, right then, it just seemed as if it had been made for only me.

> John 14:1-4, v.2 "In My Father's house are many mansions (*Literally dwellings place*); if it were not so, I would have told you. I go to prepare a place for you."
>
> Subtitle: My Place, My Space

Line: I knew I was in my place. No one could take my place.

> Mark 10:37-40, v.40 "but to sit on My right hand and on My left is not Mine to give, but it is for those for whom it is prepared."
>
> John 14:1-2 (verse 2)

Subtitle: I Had No Memory of Sin

Line: Another reason I said "you did this for me", is because I felt as if I had never sinned in my whole life.

> Eph 1:3-6, v.4 "just as He chose us in Him before the foundation of the world, that we should be holy and without blame before Him in love,"
>
> 2 Cor 5:17-19 (verse 19), Heb 10:11-18 (verse 14)

Line: I knew I had been set free from true death (sin), and it could not keep me from Jesus and the Father.

> Rom. 6:4-11, v. 4 "Therefore we were buried with Him through baptism into death, that just as Christ was raised from the dead by the glory of the Father, even so we also should walk in newness of life"
>
>> v. 8" Now if we died with Christ, we believe that we shall also live with Him"
>>
>> v. 9 "knowing that Christ, having been raised from the dead, dies no more. Death no longer has dominion over Him."
>
> 1 Cor 6:9-11 (verse 11), 2 Cor 5:17-19 (verse 18)

Line: I knew I had been set free from true death (sin), and it could not keep me from Jesus and the Father.

> Rom 8: 35-39, v.35 "Who shall separate us from the love of Christ? Shall tribulation, or distress, or persecution, or famine, or nakedness, or peril, or sword?"
>
> v. 38 "For I am persuaded that neither death nor life, nor angels nor principalities nor powers, nor things present nor things to come,"
>
> v.39 "nor height nor depth, nor any other created thing, shall be able to separate us from the love of God which is in Christ Jesus our Lord"
>
> Rev 20:12-15 (verses 14-15), Rev 21:6-8

Line: I knew I had been set free from true death (sin), and it could not keep me from Jesus and the Father.

> Rev 1:17-18, v.18" I am He who lives, and was dead, and behold, I am alive forevermore. Amen. And I have the keys of Hades and of Death."
>
> Rom 5:8-9 (verse 9), Rom 5:18-21 (verses 18-19)

Line: I had no remembrance of sinning at all.

> 2 Cor 5:17-19, v.19 "that is, that God was in Christ reconciling the world to Himself, not imputing their trespasses to them, and has committed to us the word of reconciliation."
>
> Jer 31:32-34 (verse 34), Eph 1:3-6

Line: And I knew Jesus could not have reminded me, for I was forgiven and He did not remember any of my sins.

> 1 John 1:5-10, v.9"If we confess our sins, He is faithful and just to forgive us our sins and to cleanse us from all unrighteousness."
>
> Isa 43:25-26 (verse 25), Micah 7:18-19

Line: Again I knew that I knew, that I knew.

Heb 12:22-24, v.22" But you have come to Mount Zion and to the city of the living God, the heavenly Jerusalem, to an innumerable company of angels"

v. 23 'to the general assembly and church of the firstborn who are registered in heaven, to God the Judge of all, to the spirits of just men made perfect"

v. 24" to Jesus the Mediator of the new covenant, and to the blood of sprinkling that speaks better things than that of Abel."

1 Cor 13:12-13 (verse 12)

Line: I knew I could never be separated from my Father and Jesus.

Romans 5:18-21, v.18 "Therefore, as through one man's offense judgment came to all men, resulting in condemnation, even so through one Man's righteous act the free gift came to all men, resulting in justification of life"

v. 19 "For as by one man's disobedience many were made sinners, so also by one Man's obedience many will be made righteous"

Rom 5:8-9 (verse 9)

Line: I came to understand true death is being separated from God.

Rev 20:12-15, v.14" Then Death and Hades were cast into the lake of fire. This is the second death"

v. 15 "And anyone not found written in the Book of Life was cast into the lake of fire."

Rom 8:35-39 (verses 35,38-39), Eph 1:15-23 (verses 22-23)

Line: I also came to realize that no one could hurt me in this place.

Rev 21:22-27, v.24" And the nations of those who are saved shall walk in its light, and the kings of the earth bring their glory and honor into it"

v. 25 "Its gates shall not be shut at all by day (there shall be no night there)"

v. 26" And they shall bring the glory and the honor of the nations into it"

Ps 118:6-7 (verse 6)

Chapter 5 Notes

I Have Seen Jesus

Subtitle: Jesus Is Bright

Line: All I can say is Jesus is bright.

Rev 1:12-16, v.16 "He had in His right hand seven stars, out of His mouth went a sharp two-edged sword, and His countenance (*expression, face*) was like the sun shining in its strength."

Mat 17:1-3 (verses 2-3), Acts 9:1-5 (verse 3)

Line: He was brighter than our sun on a hot sunny afternoon and yet, I was able to look at Him.

Rev 21:22-24, v. 23 "The city had no need of the sun or of the moon to shine in it, for the glory of God illuminated it. The Lamb is its light."

Acts 26:12-15 (verse 13), Rev 1:12-16 (verse 16), Rev 22:35 (verse 5)

Line: He was brighter than our sun on a hot sunny afternoon and yet, I was able to look at Him.

John 12:34-36, v.35 "Then Jesus said to them, 'A little while longer the light is with you. Walk while you have the light, lest darkness overtake you; he who walks in darkness does not know where he is going'"

v. 36 "'While you have the light, believe in the light, that you may become sons of light.' These things Jesus spoke, and departed, and was hidden from them."

Heb 1:1-4 (verse 3), 1 John 1:6-7 (verse 7)

Line: Those who were RIGHT with Him, could look at Him and would experience perfect joy.

1 John 2:28-29, v.28 " And now, little children, abide in Him, that when He appears, we may have confidence and not be ashamed before Him at His coming"

v. 29 "If you know that He is righteous, you know that everyone who practices righteousness is born of Him"

1 John 3:6-7

Line: Those who were RIGHT with Him, could look at Him and would experience perfect joy.

Eccl 2:24-25, v.25 "For God gives wisdom and knowledge and joy to a man who is good in His sight; but to the sinner He gives the work of gathering and collecting, that he may give to him who is good before God. This also is vanity and grasping for the wind."

Rom 15:13, Jude 1:24-25 (verse 24)

Line: It seemed to me that if a being were not RIGHT with Him, that being could be burned up by His brightness and would experience terror.

> Ps 94:20-23, v.23 "He has brought on them their own iniquity, and shall cut them off in their own wickedness; The LORD our God shall cut them off."
>
> Proverbs 11:5-9, Proverbs 11:20-23 (verses 20-21,23)

Line: You had to look at Him with a pure heart.

> Mat 5:6-9, v. 8" Blessed are the pure in heart, For they shall see God."
>
> 1 John 5:9-13 (verses 10 & 12)

Subtitle: His Feet

Line: They are just like John from the Bible said in Revelation 1:15.

> Rev 1:12-16, v.15 "His feet were like fine brass, as if refined in a furnace, and His voice as the sound of many waters;"
>
> Rev 2:18-19 (verse 18)

Line: He still has the wounds from where the nails pierced His feet.

> Luke 24:38-43, v.39 "Behold My hands and My feet, that it is I Myself. Handle Me and see, for a spirit does not have flesh and bones as you see I have."
>
> > v. 40 "When He had said this, He showed them His hands and His feet."

Line: It was not only that He loved me, but that it was like I was the only one He loved in all of His creation.

> Isa. 49:14-16, v.15 "Can a woman forget her nursing child, and not have compassion on the son of her womb? Surely they may forget, Yet I will not forget you."

Subtitle: His Hands

Line: Yes, you can see the nail piercings that took place in His hands.

Luke 24:38-43, v.39 "Behold My hands and My feet, that it is I Myself. Handle Me and see, for a spirit does not have flesh and bones as you see I have."

v. 40 "When He had said this, He showed them His hands and His feet."

John 20:24-27 (verses 26-27)

Subtitle: His Body

Line: Just like the Bible says in 1 John 4:7, God is love

1 John 4:12-16, v.16" And we have known and believed the love that God has for us. God is love, and he who abides in love abides in God, and God in him."

Lam 3:20-24 (verses 22-23) Rom 8:35-39 (verses 35,39)

Line: I saw what it cost for me to be there, and to have a relationship with God Almighty. I did not realize before this happened, how great was the cost of pain to the physical body of Jesus, for us to have a relationship with God.

Isa 52:13-15, v.14 "Just as many were astonished at you, So His visage was marred more than any man, And His form more than the sons of men;"

Read Isa. 52:14-15 from the NET BIBLE at bible.org Isa 53:1-2 (verse 2), Isa 53:3-6 (verse 5), Mat. 27:24-50 (26-30),

Read Mat 27:24-31 notes from the NET BIBLE at bible.org, Mark 14:41-50 (verses 41,44-45,50), Mark 15:11-15 (verse 15), Read Mark 15:16-20 notes from the NET BIBLE at bible.org,

Luke 23:22-25 (verses 23,25)

Line: In Heaven you stop looking at him with your eyes and start seeing Him from your heart. You get to see Him as He is.

> 1 John 3:1-2, v.2 "Beloved, now we are children of God; and it has not yet been revealed what we shall be, but we know that when He is revealed, we shall be like Him, for we shall see Him as He is.
>
> Eph 5:1-2 (verse 2)

Line: I came to understand that He advocates for us before the throne of God with His whole being.

> Rom 8:34 "Who is he who condemns? It is Christ who died, and furthermore is also risen, who is even at the right hand of God, who also makes intercession for us."
>
> 1 Tim 2:3-6, v.5 "For there is one God and one mediator between God and men, the man Christ Jesus"
>
> Rom 8:31-35 (verse 34), Heb 4:14-16 (verse 15)

Sub-Title: His Face

Line: His face was as if it were liquid crystal glass made up of pure love, light, and life. Jesus did have a face just like most humans, but instead it would seem to change into different human like faces.

> Luke 9:29-33, v. 29 "As He prayed, the appearance of His face was altered, and His robe became white and glistening."
>
> Mark 16:12-13 (verse 12), Luke 24:28-34 (verses 30-32)

Line: His face had the colors of the rainbow and colors I cannot describe inside of it.

Ezek 1:27-28, v.28 "Like the appearance of a rainbow in the clouds on a rainy day, so was the radiance around him. This was the appearance of the likeness of the glory of the LORD. When I saw it, I fell facedown, and I heard the voice of one speaking."

Line: They came out of Him and off of Him as the waves of the ocean flow back and forth on the shore. I was seeing the colors and yet, I was part of the colors.

Rev 4:2-3, v.3 "And the one who sat there had the appearance of jasper and carnelian. A rainbow, resembling an emerald, encircled the throne."

Line: I was seeing Jesus, and I was a part of Jesus. I was in Jesus, and Jesus was shining out of me.

John 14:19-24, v.20 "At that day you will know that I am in My Father, and you in Me, and I in you."

Acts 9:3-4 (verse 3), Rev 1:9-20 (verse 16)

Line: The brightness was around me. I was part of the brightness, and brightness was shining out of me.

Rev 21:22-23, v.23 "The city had no need of the sun or of the moon to shine in it, for the glory of God illuminated it. The Lamb is its light."

Rev 22:1-5 , v.5 "There shall be no night there: They need no lamp nor light of the sun, for the Lord God gives them light. And they shall reign forever and ever."

Eph 5:13-14 (verse 14)

Subtitle: His Head

Line: On Jesus's head was a crown that looked like the sun in all its glory.

> Rev 19:11-13, v.12 "His eyes were like a flame of fire, and on His head were many crowns. He had a name written that no one knew except Himself."
>
> Rev 6:1-2 (verse 2), Rev 14:14-16 (verse 14)

Line: This crown was really bright, with rays going up and out into the atmosphere of heaven.

> Isa 30:25-26, v.26 "Moreover the light of the moon will be as the light of the sun, And the light of the sun will be sevenfold, As the light of seven days, In the day that the LORD binds up the bruise of His people And heals the stroke of their wound."
>
> Read Isa 30:25-26 notes from the NET BIBLE at bible.org
>
> Malachi 4:2-3, v.2 "But to you who fear My name The Sun of Righteousness shall arise With healing in His wings (*warm rays*); And you shall go out And grow fat like stall-fed calves."
>
> Read Malachi 4:2-3 notes from the NET BIBLE at bible. org

Line: The rays intertwine with His hair. His hair was like John said in Revelation.

> Rev 1:9-20, v.14 "His head and hair were white like wool, as white as snow, and His eyes like a flame of fire"
>
> Daniel 7:9-10 (verse 9)

Subtitle: He Is Love

Line: Everything about Him is love.

> 1 John 4:16-17, v.16" And we have known and believed the love that God has for us. God is love, and he who abides in love abides in God, and God in him"

v. 17 "Love has been perfected among us in this: that we may have boldness in the day of judgment; because as He is, so are we in this world."

1 John 4:7-12 (verse 8)

Line: Yet you know within that He loves all, but His love for you is so personal it seems as if it is only for you.

Isa. 49:14-16, v.15 "Can a woman forget her nursing child, And not have compassion on the son of her womb? Surely they may forget, Yet I will not forget you."

Line: You know He has cared for you from the beginning and will continue to care for you forever.

Dan 7:21-27, v.22 "until the Ancient of Days came, and a judgment was made in favor of the saints of the Most High, and the time came for the saints to possess the kingdom"

v. 27 "Then the kingdom and dominion, And the greatness of the kingdoms under the whole heaven, shall be given to the people, the saints of the Most High. His kingdom is an everlasting kingdom, and all dominions shall serve and obey Him."

Rev 21:2-4, v.3 "And I heard a loud voice from heaven saying, 'Behold, the tabernacle of God is with men, and He will dwell with them, and they shall be His people. God Himself will be with them and be their God.'"

Mat 11:11-12 (verse 11)

Chapter 7 Notes

What Did I See In Heaven?

Subtitle: None

Line: When I died, I knew where to go. There was no one telling me where to go.

> John 14:1-4, v.4 "And where I go you
> know, and the way you know"

Line: Everything is alive and there is nothing dead there.

> Luke 12:32-34, v.33 "Sell what you have and give
> alms; provide yourselves money bags which do not
> grow old, a treasure in the heavens that does not fail,
> where no thief approaches nor moth destroys"
>
> Titus 1:1-3 (verse 2), Jam 1:12-13

Line: I understood then that true death was not having the Father God or Jesus or the Holy Spirit in your life.

> Rev 21:6-8, v.8 "But the cowardly, unbelieving, abominable,
> murderers, sexually immoral, sorcerers, idolaters, and
> all liars shall have their part in the lake which burns
> with fire and brimstone, which is the second death.."
>
> Rev 20:12-15 (verse 14)

Subtitle: Back From the Dead?—On the Contrary

Line: No…I was alive with the Father and Son.

> Ps 36:7-9, v. 9 "For with You is the fountain
> of life; In Your light we see light."

Mat 22:29-32, v.32 "I am the God of Abraham, the God of Isaac, and the God of Jacob'? God is not the God of the dead, but of the living."

Heb 4:11-13, v.12 "For the word of God is living and powerful, and sharper than any two-edged sword, piercing even to the division of soul and spirit, and of joints and marrow, and is a discerner of the thoughts and intents of the heart."

Line: Our God is pure life, light, and love.

LOVE

1 John 4:7-11, v. 7 "Beloved, let us love one another, for love is of God; and everyone who loves is born of God and knows God"

v. 8 "He who does not love does not know God, for God is love."

1 Cor 13:8-13 (verses 8,13), 1 John 4:15-16 (verse 16)

LIFE

Gen 2:7 "And the LORD God formed man of the dust of the ground, and breathed into his nostrils the breath of life; and man became a living being."

John 5:24-27 (verse 26)

LIGHT

Ps 36:7-9, v.9 "For with You is the fountain of life; In Your light we see light."

Ps 104:1-2, v.2 "Who cover Yourself with light as with a garment, Who stretch out the heavens like a curtain."

Ps 119:129-132, v.130 "The entrance of Your words gives light; It gives understanding to the simple."

2 Cor 4:5-6 (verse 6)

Line: As I said earlier, everything in Heaven is alive. The light-like buildings which looked like light but were not light, the landscape, and the atmosphere, were all alive.

> Rev 16:4-7, v.7 "And I heard another from the altar saying, 'Even so, Lord God Almighty, true and righteous are Your judgments.'"
>
> Read Rev 16:7 from the NET BIBLE at bible.org
>
> Rev 19:4-6,v. 5" Then a voice came from the throne, saying, 'Praise our God, all you His servants and those who fear Him, both small and great!'"

Line: As I said earlier, everything in Heaven is alive. The light-like buildings which looked like light but were not light, the landscape, and the atmosphere, were all alive.

> Rev 21:10-23, v.10 "And he carried me away in the Spirit to a great and high mountain, and showed me the great city, the holy Jerusalem, descending out of heaven from God"
>
>> v. 11 "having the glory of God. Her light was like a most precious stone, like a jasper stone, clear as crystal"
>>
>> v. 21 "The twelve gates were twelve pearls: each individual gate was of one pearl. And the street of the city was pure gold, like transparent glass"
>>
>> v. 23 "The city had no need of the sun or of the moon to shine in it, for the glory of God illuminated it. The Lamb is its light."
>
> Isa 44:21-23 (verse 23), Isa 55:11-12 (verse 12)

Line: As I said earlier, everything in Heaven is alive. The light-like building which looked like light but were not light, the landscape, and atmosphere, were all alive.

> Job 38:33-36, v.35 "Can you send out lightnings, that they may go, And say to you, "Here we are!'?"

Rev 10:3-4, v.3 "and cried with a loud voice, as when a lion roars. When he cried out, seven thunders uttered their voices."

Subtitle: Heaven Is Huge

Line: Because of coming from earth and living with death, a thought went through my thinking, "Aren't we going to run out of room in Heaven? After all there is no death and everything keeps on living?"

I Tim 6:11-14, v.13 "I urge you in the sight of God who gives life to all things, and before Christ Jesus who witnessed the good confession before Pontius Pilate."

Ezek 18:30-32, v.32 "For I have no pleasure in the death of one who dies," says the Lord GOD. "Therefore turn and live!"

Gen 1:11-13 (verse 11), Gen 1:20-24 (verses 20, 24), Gen 2:7, Ps 115:14-15 (verse 15)

Line: Heaven is big, large, huge, extensive, spacious and expanding.

Eccl 3:13-14, v.14 "I know that whatever God does, It shall be forever. Nothing can be added to it, And nothing taken from it. God does it, that men should fear before Him."

2 Cor 3:17-18 (verse 18), 2 Cor 4:16-18

Line: All I can tell people is that where God is, IS BIG!

Ps 40:5 "Many, O LORD my God, are Your wonderful works which You have done; And Your thoughts toward us cannot be recounted to You in order; If I would declare and speak of them, They are more than can be numbered."

Ps 111:2-4, Ps 115:15-16 (verse 15), Ps 123:1

Subtitle: Distance and Time

Line: If I wanted to be somewhere else in Heaven I just had to think it and I was there.

> Act 8:38-40, v.39 "Now when they came up out of the water, the Spirit of the Lord caught Philip away, so that the eunuch saw him no more; and he went on his way rejoicing."
>
> Ezek 3:11-15 (verses 12-14), John 6:15-21 (verse 21)

Line: I know I will outlast every problem that comes my way and someday soon, I will be with Jesus.

> Ps 90:3-6, v. 4 "For a thousand years in Your (God) sight are like yesterday when it is past, And like a watch in the night."
>
> Ps 102:23-28 (verse 24), 2 Pet 3:8-9 (verse 8)

Line: Why would you put time on eternity? Why do we put time on earth?

> Gen 8:20-22, v.22 "While the earth remains, seedtime and harvest, cold and heat, winter and summer, and day and night shall not cease."
>
> Gen 1:14-19 (verse 14)

Subtitle: The Atmosphere in Heaven

Line: Jesus and the Father light up everything; there is no darkness in Heaven.

> Rev 22:4-5, v.5 "There shall be no night there: They need no lamp nor light of the sun, for the Lord God gives them light. And they shall reign forever and ever."
>
> Isa 60:19-20 (verse 19), 2 Cor 4:5-6 (verse 6)

Line: It is a golden, yellow, white. An artist that I know says it sounds like sunrise colors.

Job 37:21-23, v.22 "He comes from the north as golden splendor; With God is awesome majesty."

Read Job 37:21-23 notes from the NET BIBLE at bible.org

Subtitle: The Colors in Heaven

Line: The colors of flowers here on earth are the closest to the colors I experienced in Heaven and yet, even the colors of these flowers have lost their glory compared to the colors in Heaven.

Mat 6:28-30, v.28 "So why do you worry about clothing? Consider the lilies of the field, how they grow: they neither toil nor spin"

v. 29 "and yet I say to you that even Solomon in all his glory was not arrayed like one of these"

v. 30 "Now if God so clothes the grass of the field, which today is, and tomorrow is thrown into the oven, will He not much more clothe you, O you of little faith?"

Luke 12:27-28 (verse 27)

Subtitle: Jesus' Words Are Alive

Line: His voice left Him with power and authority, but when it got to me, it was life and comfort.

Ps 107:20 "He sent his word, and healed them, and delivered them from their destructions."

Rev 1:9-20 (verses 10,12)

Line: But I felt that speaking words in Heaven was a waste of energy, or just not important.

Eccl 5:6-7, v.7 "For in the multitude of dreams and many words there is also vanity. But fear God."

Subtitle: Communication in Heaven

Line: Jesus and the Father thought something and it was transferred to me. The other beings formed a thought, and it was transferred to me.

> Acts 16:6-10, v.9 "And a vision appeared to Paul in the night. A man of Macedonia stood and pleaded with him, saying, "Come over to Macedonia and help us."
>
> > v.10 "Now after he had seen the vision, immediately we sought to go to Macedonia, concluding that the Lord had called us to preach the gospel to them."
>
> Acts 27: 9-12 (verse 10)

Line: Because everything is alive they can all communicate with you.

> Rev 4:6-8, v.7 "The first living creature was like a lion, the second living creature like a calf, the third living creature had a face like a man, and the fourth living creature was like a flying eagle"
>
> > v. 8 "The four living creatures, each having six wings, were full of eyes around and within. And they do not rest day or night, saying: Holy, Holy, Holy, Lord God Almighty, Who was and is and is to come!"
> >
> > v.9 "Whenever the living creatures give glory and honor and thanks to Him who sits on the throne, who lives forever and ever"
> >
> > v. 11 "You are worthy, O Lord, To receive glory and honor and power; For You created all things, And by Your will they exist and were created."
>
> Rev 8:12-13 (verse 13) Read Rev 8:13 from the NET BIBLE at bible.org, Rev 10:2-4, (verses 3-4), Rev16:4-7 (verse 7) Read Rev 16:7 from the NET BIBLE at bible.org

Line: Everything was RIGHT, so there was no miscommunication with each other.

> Col 4:2-6, v.5 "Walk in wisdom toward those who are outside, redeeming the time. 6 Let your speech always be with grace, seasoned with salt, that you may know how you ought to answer each one."

Line: There was nothing you would have to hide from each other. We all had pure thoughts and every thought was pure.

> Phil 4:7-9, v.8 "Finally, brethren, whatever things are true, whatever things are noble, whatever things are just, whatever things are pure, whatever things are lovely, whatever things are of good report, if there is any virtue and if there is anything praiseworthy—meditate on these things."
>
> Gen 2:23-25 (verse 25), Gen 3:4-7 (verse 7)

Line: There was a rule that you did not go into any of the heavenly creation's thoughts without first receiving permission.

> 1 Cor 6:12 "All things are lawful for me, but all things are not helpful. All things are lawful for me, but I will not be brought under the power of any."
>
> 1 Cor 8:8-9, verse 9

Line: Satan, the last being that broke the rule is no longer in heaven. Imagine the power we would have if we really understood the power of our thoughts.

> Isa 14:12-15, v. 12 "How you are fallen from heaven, O Lucifer, son of the morning! How you are cut down to the ground, You who weakened the nations!"
>
> > v. 15 "Yet you shall be brought down to Sheol, to the lowest depths of the Pit."
>
> Ezek. 28:14-17, verse 17, Luke 10:17-20, verse 18

Subtitle: Everyone and Everything Praised the Lord

Line: Every part of God's creation praises God all the time, and no one else receives praise, but only God.

> Isa 42:5-9, v.8 "I am the LORD, that is My name; And My glory I will not give to another, Nor My praise to carved images."
>
> Ex 20:2-6 (verses 3-5), Luke 4:5-8 (verse 8), Rev 21:22-27 (verse 22)

Line: When you are in Heaven you know that is what you do.

> Ps146:1-2, v.1 "Praise the LORD! Praise the LORD, O my soul!"
>
> v.2 "While I live I will praise the LORD; I will sing praises to my God while I have my being."
>
> Ps 148:1-7 (verse 1), Ps 149:1-9 (verse 1), Ps 150:1-6 (verse 2)

Line: To hear the flowers praise the Lord is wonderful. The birds sing praise to the Lord. Water praised the Lord. Mountains praised the Lord. Praise came from the atmosphere. Praise was in the atmosphere. Praise was the atmosphere. We all praised Him repeatedly, over and over again.

> Ps 148:1-14 v.1 "Praise the LORD! Praise the LORD from the heavens; Praise Him in the heights!"
>
> > v. 2 "Praise Him, all His angels; Praise Him, all His hosts!"
> >
> > v. 3 "Praise Him, sun and moon; Praise Him, all you stars of light!"
> >
> > v. 4 "Praise Him, you heavens of heavens, And you waters above the heavens!"

v. 5 "Let them praise the name of the LORD, For He commanded and they were created."

v. 6 "He also established them forever and ever; He made a decree which shall not pass away. Praise the LORD from the earth, You great sea creatures and all the depths"

v. 8 "Fire and hail, snow and clouds; Stormy wind, fulfilling His word"

v. 9 "Mountains and all hills; Fruitful trees and all cedars"

v. 10 "Beasts and all cattle; Creeping things and flying fowl"

v. 11 "Kings of the earth and all peoples; Princes and all judges of the earth"

v. 12 "Both young men and maidens; Old men and children"

v. 13 "Let them praise the name of the LORD, For His name alone is exalted; His glory is above the earth and heaven"

v. 14 "And He has exalted the horn of His people, The praise of all His saints Of the children of Israel, A people near to Him. Praise the LORD!"

Line: Writing this down reminds me of the fact, that praise did not ever leave my thinking when I was in Heaven.

John 4:23-24, v.23 "But the hour is coming, and now is, when the true worshipers will worship the Father in spirit and truth; for the Father is seeking such to worship Him."

v. 24 "God is Spirit, and those who worship Him must worship in spirit and truth."

Mat 21:15-16 (verse 16), Phil 3:17-21 (verses 20-21)

Subtitle: Our Connection In Heaven

Line: God is the connection between each and every one of His creations.

2 Cor 12:4-26, v.6 "And there are diversities of activities,
but it is the same God who works all in all"

v. 11 "But one and the same Spirit works all these things,
distributing to each one individually as He wills"

v. 12 "For as the body is one and has many
members, but all the members of that one body,
being many, are one body, so also is Christ"

v. 13 "For by one Spirit we were all baptized into one
body—whether Jews or Greeks, whether slaves or free—
and have all been made to drink into one Spirit"

v. 18 "But now God has set the members, each
one of them, in the body just as He pleased"

v. 20 "But now indeed there are many
members, yet one body"

v. 25 "that there should be no schism in the body, but that
the members should have the same care for one another"

v. 26 "And if one member suffers, all the
members suffer with it; or if one member is
honored, all the members rejoice with it"

Rom 15:5-6, Col 2:1-3 (verses 2-3)

Subtitle: Relating My Experience To You

Line: There is no sin to corrupt what God has made.

Rev 21:22-27, v.27 "But there shall by no means enter it anything that defiles, or causes an abomination or a lie, but only those who are written in the Lamb's Book of Life."

Chapter 9 Notes

The True Gatekeeper of Heaven

Subtitle: None

Line: I came to understand who the real gatekeeper of Heaven is. It is Jesus, only Jesus.

> John 6:38-40, v.40 "And this is the will of Him who sent Me, that everyone who sees the Son and believes in Him may have everlasting life; and I will raise him up at the last day."
>
> John 10:14-16 (verses 15-16), 2 Peter 3:8-9 (verse 9)

Subtitle: I Looked Into Jesus' Eyes

Line: The eyes of Jesus are like flames of fire with changing colors of red, orange, blue, green, yellow, and many other colors within them. John said in Revelation 1:14 that, "His eyes (are) like a flame of fire"

> Rev 1:12-14, v.14 "His head and hair were white like wool, as white as snow, and His eyes like a flame of fire"
>
> Rev 2:18-19 (verse 18), Rev 19:11-14 (verse 12)

Line: I saw in the eyes of Jesus that He wanted everyone in Heaven who is still alive on this earth.

> 1 Tim 2:1-4, v.1 "Therefore I exhort first of all that supplications, prayers, intercessions, and giving of thanks be made for all men"
>
>> v. 3 "For this is good and acceptable in the sight of God our Savior"
>>
>> v. 4 "who desires all men to be saved and to come to the knowledge of the truth"
>
> Isa 55:6-7 (verse 7), Luke 5:29-32 (verses 31-32)

Subtitle: He Loves Us No Matter What

Line: Then His eyes looked at me with the fiery red flame and said, "WHO ARE YOU TO NULIFY WHAT I HAD DONE!"

Rom 5:6-11, v.6 "For when we were still without strength, in due time Christ died for the ungodly"

v. 8 "But God demonstrates His own love toward us, in that while we were still sinners, Christ died for us"

v. 9 "Much more then, having now been justified by His blood, we shall be saved from wrath through Him"

v. 10 "For if when we were enemies we were reconciled to God through the death of His Son, much more, having been reconciled, we shall be saved by His life"

v. 11 "And not only that, but we also rejoice in God through our Lord Jesus Christ, through whom we have now received the reconciliation."

Rom 4:24-25 (verse 25), Rom 6:3-10 (verses 4,8-10), Gal 1:3-5 (verse 4), Eph 2:1-10 (verses 1,4-6,8,10)

Chapter 11 Notes

Jesus Wants All People Saved

Subtitle: None

Line: He was strategizing with some beings that were standing in a half circle around Him.

Pr 19:20-21, v.21 "There are many plans in a man's heart, nevertheless the LORD's counsel—that will stand."

2 Chro 20:13-17 (verses 14-17), Isa 9:6-7 (verse 6), Read Isa 9:6-7 notes from the NET BIBLE at bible.org, Isa 55:8-9

Line: He was communicating His plans to them of how to get more people on this earth to know Him as Lord and Savior.

> Mat 9:35-38, v.36 "But when He saw the multitudes, He was moved with compassion for them, because they were weary and scattered, like sheep having no shepherd."
>
> > v.37 "Then He said to His disciples, "The harvest truly is plentiful, but the laborers are few."
> >
> > v. 38 "Therefore pray the Lord of the harvest to send out laborers into His harvest."
>
> Mat 18:10-14 (verses 10-11,14), Luke 15:1-10 (verses 12,7,10), John 6:35-47 (verses 37,39-40,44,47-48)

Line: God is using everything that he can to get people to know Jesus as Lord and Savior.

> Ezek 18:30-32, v.32 "For I have no pleasure in the death of one who dies," says the Lord GOD. "Therefore turn and live!"
>
> Ps 111:9, John 6:43-44 (verse 44)

Line: He is looking for people on earth to work with Him in getting other people to know who He is.

> Ezek 22:30-31, v.30 "So I sought for a man among them who would make a wall, and stand in the gap before Me on behalf of the land, that I should not destroy it; but I found no one."
>
> 1 Sam 13:13-14 (verse 14), Dan 9:2-3 (verse 3)

Line: Jesus is urging all of mankind to press into the Kingdom of God.

> Luke 16:16-17, v.16 "The law and the prophets were until John. Since that time the kingdom of God has been preached, and everyone is pressing into it."
>
> Eph 4:1-3 (verses 1,3), 1 Thes 2:10-12 (verse 11)

Line: We are so very important to Him!

> Mat 10:29-31, v.30 "But the very hairs
> of your head are all numbered."
>
> > v. 31" Do not fear therefore; you are of
> > more value than many sparrows."
>
> Luke 12:4-7 (verse 6), Rom 8: 18-30 (verse 30)

Line: Because of this, I understood just how important we that are on earth are to Him.

> Dan 4:1-3, v.4 "I Nebuchadnezzar the king, to all peoples, nations, and languages that dwell in all the earth: Peace be multiplied to you. I thought it good to declare the signs and wonders that the Most High God has worked for me."
>
> John 3:1-18 (verses 16-17), 1 Tim 2:1-4

Subtitle: Heavenly Interventions

Line: However, when I look throughout the New Testament there is more than one occurrence where Jesus sends angels on what I call "heavenly interventions" to get people saved.

> Acts 8:26-40, v.26 "Now an angel of the Lord spoke to Philip, saying, "Arise and go toward the south along the road which goes down from Jerusalem to Gaza." This is desert."
>
> Acts 10:1-48, v.3 "About the ninth hour of the
> day he saw clearly in a vision an angel of God
> coming in and saying to him, 'Cornelius!'"
>
> Acts 12:5-19 (verse 7)

Line: As soon as someone turns to God in his or her heart, Jesus is right there.

> Dan 10:10-21, v.12" Then he said to me, 'Do not fear, Daniel, for from the first day that you set your heart to understand, and to humble yourself before your God, your words were heard; and I have come because of your words.'"
>
> **Line:** I tell others that there are many people in Heaven that we perhaps did not think would be there.

> Rom 14:1-4, v.4 "Who are you to judge another's servant? To his own master he stands or falls. Indeed, he will be made to stand, for God is able to make him stand."
>
> Mat 22:1-14, (verses 8-9), John 10:22-30 (verses 27-28)

Line: There are also those who we thought would be in Heaven, but are not.

> Mat 22:1-13, v.11 "But when the king came in to see the guests, he saw a man there who did not have on a wedding garment."
>
> v.12 "So he said to him, 'Friend, how did you come in here without a wedding garment? And he was speechless."
>
> v. 13 "Then the king said to the servants, 'Bind him hand and foot, take him away, and cast him into outer darkness; there will be weeping and gnashing of teeth.'"
>
> Mat 23:27-28, Rom 11:19-36 (verses 20-21)

Line: As it says in Romans chapter 10, God is looking at a person's heart —not just what they say or do.

> Rom 10:1-13, v.9 "that if you confess with your mouth the Lord Jesus and believe in your heart that God has raised Him from the dead, you will be saved"
>
> v. 10 "For with the heart one believes unto righteousness, and with the mouth confession is made unto salvation."
>
> Luke 6:46-49 (verse 48), John 2:23-25 (verses 24-25)

Line: Heaven is a place where everything is right and everyone has the right to be in a place of rightness.

> Rom 10:1-13, v.4 "For Christ is the end of the law for righteousness to everyone who believes".
>
> Ps 119:137-144 (verse 144), 2 Cor 5:12-21 (verse 21)

Line: Everything there is alive and everyone has a right to live with God forever.

> John 3:1-21, v.17 "For God did not send His Son into the world to condemn the world, but that the world through Him might be saved."
>
> John 5:24-30 (verse 24), John 17:20-26 (verse 24)

Subtitle: The Army of God

Line: There is a heavenly unit and earthly unit, but they are the same army of God.

> 1 Sam 17:1-58, v.45 "Then David said to the Philistine, 'You come to me with a sword, with a spear, and with a javelin. But I come to you in the name of the LORD of hosts, the God of the armies of Israel, whom you have defied.'"
>
> > v. 46 "This day the LORD will deliver you into my hand, and I will strike you and take your head from you. And this day I will give the carcasses of the camp of the Philistines to the birds of the air and the wild beasts of the earth, that all the earth may know that there is a God in Israel."
> >
> > Gen 3:1-24 (verse 24), Eph 6:10-12 (verse 12)

Line: The heavenly unit is made up of the angels of God.

> Mat 26:48-54, v.53 "Or do you think that I cannot now pray to My Father, and He will provide Me with more than twelve legions (72 Thousand Angels) of angels?"
>
> 2 King 6:8-23 (verse 17), Dan 4:34-36 (verse 35)

Line: They understood whose government they belong to.

Dan 7:9-14, v.13 "I was watching in the night visions, And behold, One like the Son of Man, Coming with the clouds of heaven! He came to the Ancient of Days, and they brought Him near before Him."

v. 14 "Then to Him was given dominion and glory and a kingdom, That all peoples, nations, and languages should serve Him. His dominion is an everlasting dominion, which shall not pass away, And His kingdom the one Which shall not be destroyed."

Dan 2:24-45 (verses 44-45), Mat 18;10-14 (verse 10)

Line: They understood whose Kingdom they work for.

Mat 13:36-43, v.41 "The Son of Man will send out His angels, and they will gather out of His kingdom all things that offend, and those who practice lawlessness,"

v. 42 "and will cast them into the furnace of fire. There will be wailing and gnashing of teeth."

Heb 12:25-29 (verse 28), Rev 19:11-16 (verse 14)

Line: When Jesus would communicate to them, they showed great AWE or respect.

1 Pet 3:18-22, v.22 "who has gone into heaven and is at the right hand of God, angels and authorities and powers having been made subject to Him."

Ps 89:5-7 (verse 5), Isa 6:1-3 (verse 2)

Line: I wanted to be with His creation that respected Him for who He is. He is the King of Kings and Lord of Lords.

Rev 19:11-16, v.16" And He has on His robe and on His thigh a name written: KING OF KINGS AND LORD OF LORDS."

Pr 19:12-25 (verse 23), Phil 2:5-11 (verses 9-11)

Line: I witnessed how those heavenly creatures would bow when they came before the Lord and bow before they left Him, and then back out as they left.

> Ps 89:1-18, v.7 "God is greatly to be feared (respect) in the assembly of the saints (Angels), And to be held in reverence by all those around Him."
>
> Zech 6:1-8 (verses 5-7)

Line: They left quickly to complete the assignment that He sent them on.

> Joel 2:5-11, v.7 "They (Angels) run like mighty men, They climb the wall like men of war; Every one marches in formation, And they do not break ranks."
>
> > v. 8" They do not push one another; Every one marches in his own column. Though they lunge between the weapons, They are not cut down."
> >
> > Dan 10:10-24 (verse 11), Luke 2:8-14, (verses 9-10,13-14)

Line: He sent them on.

> Mat 24:29-31, v.31 "And He will send His angels with a great sound of a trumpet, and they will gather together His elect from the four winds, from one end of heaven to the other."
>
> Luke 1:1-25 (verse 19)

Line: ...and I did not see one of them question anything He commanded them to do.

> Jude 1:5-10, v.9 "Yet Michael the archangel, in contending with the devil, when he disputed about the body of Moses, dared not bring against him a reviling accusation, but said, "The Lord rebuke you!"
>
> Luke 1:5-25 (verses 19-20)

Line: This heavenly unit was sent to fight in the heavenlies.

2 Sam 5:17-25, v.23 "Therefore David inquired of the LORD, and He said, 'You shall not go up; circle around behind them, and come upon them in front of the mulberry trees.'"

v. 24 "And it shall be, when you hear the sound of marching in the tops of the mulberry trees, then you shall advance quickly. For then the LORD will go out before you to strike the camp of the Philistines."

Dan 10:10-21 (verse 13), Rev 12:7-12 (verse 7)

Line: They were fighting evil spirits that belong to Satan's army.

Eph 6:10-20, v.12 "For we do not wrestle against flesh and blood, but against principalities, against powers, against the rulers of the darkness of this age, against spiritual hosts of wickedness in the heavenly places."

Dan 10:1-21 (verses 20-21)

Line: I knew that it was prayer that determined these heavenly movements.

Mat 9:35-38, v.37 "Then He said to His disciples, 'The harvest truly is plentiful, but the laborers are few.'"

v. 38 "Therefore pray the Lord of the harvest to send out laborers into His harvest."

2 Chr 7:12-21 (verses 14-15), Mat 6:5-13 (verses 8-10)

Line: Then, there was the earthly unit.

1 Sam 17:1-58, v.26 "Then David spoke to the men who stood by him, saying, "What shall be done for the man who kills this Philistine and takes away the reproach from Israel? For who is this uncircumcised Philistine, that he should defy the armies of the living God?"

> v.45 "Then David said to the Philistine, 'You come to me with a sword, with a spear, and with a javelin. But I come to you in the name of the LORD of hosts, the God of the armies of Israel, whom you have defied.'"

Eph 6:10-20 (verses 10-11)

Line: When Jesus told me to "Go Back", I knew within he was saying, "I need you on earth more than here," and I left as a soldier going to war.

Mat 28:16-20, v.19 "Go therefore and make disciples of all the nations, baptizing them in the name of the Father and of the Son and of the Holy Spirit,"

> v. 20 "teaching them to observe all things that I have commanded you; and lo, I am with you always, even to the end of the age." Amen.

Col 4:1-10 (verse 2)

Line: I knew that it would be for a short time and that my life on this earth would be short lived.

Ps 39:4-6, v.5 "Indeed, You have made my days as handbreadths, and my age is as nothing before You; Certainly every man at his best state is but vapor. Selah"

Phil 3:17-20 (verse 20), Heb 11:13-16 (verse 13)

Line: I know what the heart of God is. It is to get people saved and to get people to live with Him forever.

John 3:1-12, v.16 "For God so loved the world that He gave His only begotten Son, that whoever believes in Him should not perish but have everlasting life."

2 Cor 12-20 (verse 14), 1 John 3:1-3 (verse 1)

Subtitle: God's Army On Earth

Line: First of all, this unit is composed of people who love God with all their being.

> Ps 31:21-24, v.23 "Oh, love the LORD, all you His saints! For the LORD preserves the faithful, and fully repays the proud person."
>
> Mat 22:34-40, v.37 "Jesus said to him, 'You shall love the LORD your God with all your heart, with all your soul, and with all your mind'".
>
> John 14:15-18 (verse 15)

Line: These are they that say Jesus is Lord and Savior.

> Mat 16:24-27, v.24 "Then Jesus said to His disciples, 'If anyone desires to come after Me, let him deny himself, and take up his cross, and follow Me.'"
>
> Col 3:12-17 (verses 12-13)

Line: They know who sent them.

> John 15:9-17, v.16 "You did not choose Me, but I chose you and appointed you that you should go and bear fruit, and that your fruit should remain, that whatever you ask the Father in My name He may give you."
>
> > v. 17" These things I command you, that you love one another".
>
> Mat 23:1-36 (verses 11-12), 1 Thess 3:11-13 (verse 11)

Line: These have come to an understanding of His authority and whose authority they have.

> John 14:12-14, v.12 "Most assuredly, I say to you, he who believes in Me (Jesus), the works that I do he will do also; and greater works than these he will do, because I go to My Father."

v. 13 "And whatever you ask in My name, that I will do, that the Father may be glorified in the Son."

v. 14 "If you ask anything in My name, I will do it."

Line: They know there is a war going on with Satan and his fallen angels.

Eph 6:10-20, v.11 "Put on the whole armor of God, that you may be able to stand against the wiles of the devil."

v. 12 "For we do not wrestle against flesh and blood, but against principalities, against powers, against the rulers of the darkness of this age, against spiritual hosts of wickedness in the heavenly places."

Mat 10:34-39 (verse 34), 1 Pet 5:6-11 (verse 8)

Line: They know their weapons and use them in battles they encounter.

2 Cor 10:1-6, v.3 "For though we walk in the flesh, we do not war according to the flesh."

v. 4 "For the weapons of our warfare are not carnal but mighty in God for pulling down strongholds,"

v.5 "casting down arguments and every high thing that exalts itself against the knowledge of God, bringing every thought into captivity to the obedience of Christ"

Mat 10:1-4 (verse 1), Rom 12:3-8 (verse 3)

Line: They have a great understanding of whose government and kingdom they are under and belong to.

Eph 2:19-22, v.20 "having been built on the foundation of the apostles and prophets, Jesus Christ Himself being the chief cornerstone,"

v. 21 "in whom the whole building, being fitted together, grows into a holy temple in the Lord,"

v. 22 "in whom you also are being built together for a dwelling place of God in the Spirit."

Ps 47:8-9 (verse 8), John 12:44-50 (verses 49-50)

Line: They spend a lot of time with the Father in His Word (Bible) and in prayer.

Mat 26:36-46, v.41 "Watch and pray, lest you enter into temptation. The spirit indeed is willing, but the flesh is weak."

2 Tim 2:14-26, v.15" Be diligent to present yourself approved to God, a worker who does not need to be ashamed, rightly dividing the word of truth."

1 Thess 5:12-20, v.17 "pray without ceasing,"

Line: They are able to hear His voice when He commands them to do something.

John 10:20-30, v.27" My sheep hear My voice, and I know them, and they follow Me."

Eph 2:14-18 (verse 18)

Line: They understand that when Jesus or the Father through the Holy Spirit asks them to do something for the Kingdom, it is a command and not a request.

1 John 3:16-24, v.22 "And whatever we ask we receive from Him, because we keep His commandments and do those things that are pleasing in His sight."

v. 23 "And this is His commandment: that we should believe on the name of His Son Jesus Christ and love one another, as He gave us commandment."

v.24 "Now he who keeps His commandments abides in Him, and He in him. And by this we know that He abides in us, by the Spirit whom He has given us."

John 15:9-17 (verse 14), John 10:7-21 (verse 18)

Line: These have come to know their purpose on this earth and accept it.

Heb 10:19-25, v.24 "And let us consider one another in order to stir up love and good works,"

v. 25 "not forsaking the assembling of ourselves together, as is the manner of some, but exhorting one another, and so much the more as you see the Day approaching."

Rom 15:1-6 (verse 2), Gal 6:1-5 (verses 1-2)

Line: They are willing to lose their lives here on earth for Him.

John 12:20-26, v.25 "He who loves his life will lose it, and he who hates his life in this world will keep it for eternal life."

Mat 19:20-22 (verse 21), Mat 20:24-28 (verses 26-27)

Line: They know that they are part of a bigger army and have a God that will always be with them.

Mat 18:15-20, v.20 "For where two or three are gathered together in My name, I am there in the midst of them".

Ps 78:12-16 (verse 12), Mat 11:25-30 (verse 30)

Line: I came to understand that I was not being sent out alone with a heavy load.

Rom 8:31-37, v.31 "What then shall we say to these things? If God is for us, who can be against us?"

v. 32 "He who did not spare His own Son, but delivered Him up for us all, how shall He not with Him also freely give us all things?"

Heb 12:1-2, Heb 13:1-6 (verses 5-6)

Chapter 13 Notes

What Jesus Told Me About Our Churches

Subtitle: Two Spirits In The Church

Line: First, He let me know that there are two spirits or attitudes in our churches today.

> 1 John 4:4-6, v.6 "We are of God. He who knows God hears us; he who is not of God does not hear us. By this we know the spirit of truth and the spirit of error."

Line: He let me know that His church is not one denomination against another.

> Eph 6:10-20, v.12 "For we do not wrestle against flesh and blood, but against principalities, against powers, against the rulers of the darkness of this age, against spiritual hosts of wickedness in the heavenly places."

Line: Chapter 10 in Romans contains the scripture that tells EVERYONE what they must do to enter the gates of Heaven.

> Rom 10:8-10, v.9 "that if you confess with your mouth the Lord Jesus and believe in your heart that God has raised Him from the dead, you will be saved."
>
> v. 10" For with the heart one believes unto righteousness, and with the mouth confession is made unto salvation."

Line: If a person will confess Jesus as Lord and believe that He was raised from the dead, Jesus will come into their heart and fill it with an overwhelming love for God and others.

> 1 John 4:17-19, v.17 "Love has been perfected among us in this: that we may have boldness in the day of judgment; because as He is, so are we in this world."
>
> 1 John 3:1-3 (verse 3), 1 John 3:10-15 (verse 11)

Subtitle: We Are One Body

Line: Believers in Christ do meet in different buildings, but God sees everyone who has accepted Jesus as Lord and Savor as in His church.

> 1 John 4:1-3, v.2 "By this you know the Spirit of God: Every spirit that confesses that Jesus Christ has come in the flesh is of God"
>
> > v. 3 "and every spirit that does not confess that Jesus Christ has come in the flesh is not of God. And this is the spirit of the Antichrist, which you have heard was coming, and is now already in the world."
> >
> > Mat 16:13-20 (verse 18), Acts 2:46-47 (verse 47), Eph 5:2232 (verse 27), 1 John 4:1-3 (verse 2)

Line: He wants each of us to belong to a local body of believers so we can build each other up for the work He has set before us.

> Heb 10:19-15, v. 24 "And let us consider one another in order to stir up love and good works,"
>
> > v. 25 "not forsaking the assembling of ourselves together, as is the manner of some, but exhorting one another, and so much the more as you see the Day approaching."
>
> Eph 4:11-16 (verse 11), 1 John 1:1-10 (verses 3,7)

Line: I came to understand that it is a part of the government of God, as a local body of those who believe in Jesus as the Son of God and have made Him Lord and Savior of their lives.

> 1 John 4:1-3, v. 2 "By this you know the Spirit of God: Every spirit that confesses that Jesus Christ has come in the flesh is of God,"
>
> > v. 3 "and every spirit that does not confess that Jesus Christ has come in the flesh is not of God. And this is the spirit of the Antichrist, which you have heard was coming, and is now a already in the world."

1 John 3:4-10 (verse 9), 1 John 2:3-6 (verse 5), 1 John 2:2023 (verse 23)

Line: These are people that believe that God the Father, sent His son into the world to save it, to save you, to save people.

John 3:1-21, v.17 "For God did not send His Son into the world to condemn the world, but that the world through Him might be saved."

Eph 2:11-22 (verse 13)

Line: Those that believe that the Holy Spirit, Jesus and the Father are one and that there is only one true God, the one who made man, not a man-made God.

John 14:15-18, v. 17 "the Spirit of truth, whom the world cannot receive, because it neither sees Him nor knows Him; but you know Him, for He dwells with you and will be in you."

v. 18 "I will not leave you orphans; I will come to you."

John 17:6-19, v. 11 "Now I am no longer in the world, but these are in the world, and I come to You. Holy Father, keep through Your name those whom You have given Me, that they may be one as We are."

John 1:1-5 (verse 1), John 10:25-30 (verse 30), Col 2:8-10 (verse 9)

Line: Those that believe that Holy Spirit, Jesus and the Father are one and that there is only one true God, the one who made man, not a man-made God.

Gen 1:26-28, v. 27" So God created man in His own image; in the image of God He created him; male and female He created them."

Gen 5:1-5 (verse 2), 1 Cor 11:1-16 (verse 12)

Line: Those that believe that Holy Spirit, Jesus and the Father are one and that there is only one true God, the one who made man, not a man-made God.

> Rom 1:18-25, v. 22 "Professing to be wise, they became fools,"
>
> > v.23 "and changed the glory of the incorruptible God into an image made like corruptible man—and birds and four-footed animals and creeping things."
>
> Ps 106:19-21 (verse 19), Isa 19:1-16 (verse 1)

Line: Everyone who believes that Jesus is the Christ has been fathered by God (1John 5:1).

> 1 John 5:1-5, v. 1 "Whoever believes that Jesus is the Christ is born of God, and everyone who loves Him who begot also loves him who is begotten of Him."
>
> > v. 4 "For whatever is born of God overcomes the world. And this is the victory that has overcome the world our faith."
>
> 1 John 2: 18-29 (verses 23,29)

Line: He wants us to follow His Government/Kingdom rules on how to confront, correct or deal with each other.

> Mat 18:15-35, v. 15 "Moreover if your brother sins against you, go and tell him his fault between you and him alone. If he hears you, you have gained your brother."
>
> > v. 16 "But if he will not hear, take with you one or two more, that 'by the mouth of two or three witnesses every word may be established.'"
>
> 1 Cor 6:1-11 (verse 1)

Subtitle: The First Spirit

Line: This spirit seeks to serve others first.

> Mart 25:34-40, v. 40 "And the King will answer and say to them, 'Assuredly, I say to you, inasmuch as you did it to one of the least of these My brethren, you did it to Me.'"
>
> Phil 2:5-8 (verse 8)

Line: Those who have this spirit keep God's Word at all cost.

> John 14:22-31, v. 23 "Jesus answered and said to him, 'If anyone loves Me, he will keep My word; and My Father will love him, and We will come to him and make Our home with him.'"
>
> John 8:31-32 (verse 31), Heb 10:23-25 (verse 23)

Line: They have not denied His Name.

> 2 Tim 2:11-15, v. 11 "This is a faithful saying: For if we died with Him, We shall also live with Him."
>
> Mat 10:23-33 (verse 32), 1 Tim 1:18-19 (verse 19)

Line: They also know His Word is the Word of perseverance, in which He keeps them from the hour of testing.

> 1 John 5:1-19, v. 4 "For whatever is born of God overcomes the world. And this is the victory that has overcome the world— our faith."
>
> Ps 73:25-26 (verse 26), Isa 40:27-31 (verse 31)

Line: They also know His Word is the Word of perseverance, in which He keeps them from the hour of testing.

> Heb 13:1-6, v. 5 "Let your conduct be without covetousness; be content with such things as you have. For He Himself has said, 'I will never leave you nor forsake you.'"
>
> Rom 8:31-35 (verse 35), 1 John 5:18-21 (verse 18)

Line: They are holding fast to what they know.

> Luke 12:8-12, v. 8 "Also I say to you, whoever confesses Me before men, him the Son of Man also will confess before the angels of God."
>
> John 6:22-27 (verse 27), 1 Tim 6:18-19 (verse 19)

Line: Those that have this spirit have a crown that no one can take from them. They can give it away, but no one can take it.

> 1 Tim 4:6-8, v. 8 "Finally, there is laid up for me the crown of righteousness, which the Lord, the righteous Judge, will give to me on that Day, and not to me only but also to all who have loved His appearing."
>
> Ps 5:11-12 (verse 12), Mat 5:5-10 (verse 10)

Line: They are truly overcoming all that they face on this earth.

> Luke 12:46-49, v. 48 "He is like a man building a house, who dug deep and laid the foundation on the rock. And when the flood arose, the stream beat vehemently against that house, and could not shake it, for it was founded on the rock."
>
> Ps 37:27-28 (verse 28), Rom 15:1-6 (verse 4)

Line: They will be made a pillar in God's temple and will not go out from the temple of God.

> John 12:24-26, v. 25 "He who loves his life will lose it, and he who hates his life in this world will keep it for eternal life."
>
> John 14:1-6 (verse 3), Luke 12:35-38 (verse 37)

Line: They will have the name of God written on them along with the name of the city of God on them.

> Rev 14:1-5, v. 1 "Then I looked, and behold, a Lamb standing on Mount Zion, and with Him one hundred and forty-four thousand, having His Father's name written on their foreheads."

Subtitle: The Second Spirit

Line: It has everything to do with a person's heart.

> John 2:23-25, v. 25 "and had no need that anyone should testify of man, for He knew what was in man."
>
> Ps 69:5-12 (verse 5), Mat 15:15-21 (verse 19)

Line: This Laodicean spirit is neither cold nor hot.

> Mat 15:1-9, v. 8 "These people draw near to Me with their mouth, and honor Me with their lips, but their heart is far from Me."
>
> > v.9 "And in vain they worship Me, Teaching as doctrines the commandments of men."
>
> Cor 10:14-22 (verse 21)

Line: Because they are lukewarm He is going to spit (Greek: vomit) them out of His mouth.

> Lev 18:1-30, v. 28 "lest the land vomit you out also when you defile it, as it vomited out the nations that were before you."
>
> Ps 119:17-27 (verse 21)

Line: They that have this spirit say they are rich, wealthy and need nothing.

> Jer 9:23-24, v. 23 "Thus says the LORD: 'Let not the wise man glory in his wisdom, Let not the mighty man glory in his might, Nor let the rich man glory in his riches;"
>
> Ps 49:5-12 (verses 6-7), 1 John 2:15-17 (verse 15)

Line: Jesus said they do not know they are really wretched, miserable, poor, blind and naked.

Eccl 4:1-7, v. 8 "There is one alone, without companion: He has neither son nor brother. Yet there is no end to all his labors, Nor is his eye satisfied with riches. But he never asks, 'For whom do I toil and deprive myself of good?' This also is vanity and a grave misfortune."

1 Tim 6:17-19 (verse 17)

Line: Their problem is God knows their heart, He knows which spirit they have.

1 Sam 16:6-13, v. 7 "But the LORD said to Samuel, 'Do not look at his appearance or at his physical stature, because I have refused him. For the LORD does not see as man sees; for man looks at the outward appearance, but the LORD looks at the heart.'"

Mat 15:15-20 (verse 18), Mark 10:5-9 (verse 5)

Line: Then Jesus goes on to tell them to buy gold from Him that has been refined by fire.

Pr 16:8-12, v. 8 "Better is a little with righteousness, than vast revenues without justice."

Heb 13:1-6 (verses 5-6)

Line: He wants them to have white garments so that they can clothe themselves.

Rev 19:11-16, v. 14 "And the armies in heaven, clothed in fine linen, white and clean, followed Him on white horses."

Isa 1:17-20 (verse 18), John 8:1-12 (verse 12)

Line: He wants them to have their eyes to be opened so that they can see.

Pr 30:11-15, v. 12 "There is a generation that is pure in its own eyes, Yet is not washed from its filthiness."

v. 13 "There is a generation—oh, how lofty are their eyes! And their eyelids are lifted up."

Read Rev 3:18 notes from the NET BIBLE at bible.org

Line: Because HE LOVES THEM, he reproves and disciplines them who have this spirit.

> Heb 12:5-11, v. 5" And you have forgotten the exhortation which speaks to you as to sons: 'My son, do not despise the chastening of the LORD, Nor be discouraged when you are rebuked by Him;"
>
> > v.6 "For whom the LORD loves He chastens, and scourges every son whom He receives."
>
> I Cor 11:27-34 (verse 32)

Line: Jesus is knocking on the door to their spirit, waiting for them to open their spirit to Him.

> Isa 54:1-16, v. 5 "For your Maker is your husband, The LORD of hosts is His name; and your Redeemer is the Holy One of Israel; He is called the God of the whole earth".

Subtitle: The Church Can Change Our Nations

Line: The other thing Jesus communicated to me while I was in Heaven was "How the church down here on earth goes, so does a nation."

> 2 Chron 6:1-42, v. 34 "When Your people go out to battle against their enemies, wherever You send them, and when they pray to You toward this city which You have chosen and the temple which I have built for Your name,"
>
> > v. 35 "then hear from heaven their prayer and their supplication, and maintain their cause."
>
> Gen 41:1-57 (verse 28)

Line: He really does want His people who are called by His name to humble themselves, pray, seek His face and turn from their individual wicked ways.

2 Chron 7:12-22, v. 14 "if My people who are called by My name will humble themselves, and pray and seek My face, and turn from their wicked ways, then I will hear from heaven, and will forgive their sin and heal their land."

Gen 18:1-33 (verse 32), Dan 4:1-37 (verses 1-3)

Line: If His people will do this, their nation will turn around.

Jonah 3:1-10, v. 5 "So the people of Nineveh believed God, proclaimed a fast, and put on sackcloth, from the greatest to the least of them."

v. 10 "Then God saw their works, that they turned from their evil way; and God relented from the disaster that He had said He would bring upon them, and He did not do it."

2 Chron 20:1-30 (verses 3,15,27)

Line: We that believe in Jesus as Lord and Savior can change our nations around, whether it is the United States, Peru, France, England, Canada, China, Uganda, Israel, or any other nation.

1 Tim 2:1-7, v. 1 "Therefore I exhort first of all that supplications, prayers, intercessions, and giving of thanks be made for all men,"

v. 2 "for kings and all who are in authority, that we may lead a quiet and peaceable life in all godliness and reverence."

v. 3 "For this is good and acceptable in the sight of God our Savior,"

v. 4 "who desires all men to be saved and to come to the knowledge of the truth."

Chapter 14 Notes

What God Does With Our Prayers

Subtitle: 2 Corinthians 5:8 (NKJV)
...to be absent from the body and
to be present with the Lord.

Line: I knew where to go and no one had to tell me where to go.

John 14:1-6, v. 3 "And if I go and prepare a place for you, I will come again and receive you to Myself; that where I am, there you may be also."

v. 4 "And where I go you know, and the way you know."

Phil 1:19-26 (verse 21)

Line: As 2 Corinthians says, I was absent from my body, and I was in the presence of my Lord.

2 Cor 5:1-8, v. 8 "We are confident, yes, well pleased rather to be absent from the body and to be present with the Lord."

1 Cor 15:50-54 (verses 51-52)

Line: Yet the prayers of people that were praying for me and other prayers were moving faster than I was.

Dan 10:10-21, v. 12 "Then he said to me, 'Do not fear, Daniel, for from the first day that you set your heart to understand, and to humble yourself before your God, your words were heard; and I have come because of your words.'"

1 John 5:14-15 (verse 14)

Subtitle: Two Types of Prayers

Line: One type were prayers from people that had prayed a prayer and understood the authority they had when they prayed the prayer.

> Mark 11:20-24, v. 24 "Therefore I say to you, whatever things you ask when you pray, believe that you receive them, and you will have them."
>
> John 15:1-8 (verse 7), 1 John 5:14-15 (verse 14)

Line: They were praying in faith from their hearts.

> Ps 34:1-22, v. 18" The LORD is near to those who have a broken heart, and saves such as have a contrite spirit."
>
> **Line:** They were praying according to a verse in the Bible that they had understood the meaning of.
>
> Heb 4:8-13, v. 12 "For the word of God is living and powerful, and sharper than any two-edged sword, piercing even to the division of soul and spirit, and of joints and marrow, and is a discerner of the thoughts and intents of the heart."
>
> Eph 1:15-22 (verse 17)

Line: They were praying the will of God for me and others.

> Rom 8:18-30, v. 26 "Likewise the Spirit also helps in our weaknesses. For we do not know what we should pray for as we ought, but the Spirit Himself makes intercession for us with groanings which cannot be uttered."
>
> > v. 27 "Now He who searches the hearts knows what the mind of the Spirit is, because He makes intercession for the saints according to the will of God."
>
> Mat 6:5-14 (verse 10), Mat 21:19-22 (verse 22)

Line: And they knew that God would answer the prayer with His power.

1 John 3:16-23, v. 22 "And whatever we ask we receive from Him, because we keep His commandments and do those things that are pleasing in His sight."

John 9:13-34 (verse 31)

Line: We are told to pray His will here on earth in Matthew 6:10.

Mat 6:5-14, v. 9 "In this manner, therefore, pray: Our Father in heaven, Hallowed be Your name."

v. 10 "Your kingdom come. Your will be done on earth as it is in heaven."

Luke 11:1-4 (verse 2)

Line: But also remember my wife's sacrifice and battle to get that outcome.

Luke 18:1-8, v. 1 "Then He spoke a parable to them, that men always ought to pray and not lose heart,"

Ezek 22:23-30 (verse 30), Mat 7:7-12 (verse 7)

Line: They had faith in what they prayed, not really understanding what they were fully praying for.

Eph 3:14-21, v. 20 "Now to Him who is able to do exceedingly abundantly above all that we ask or think, according to the power that works in us"

Gen 19:27-29 (verse 29)

Subtitle: Where Our Prayers Go

Line: Not only did they go to the Father God, they went inside of Him.

Rev 8:1-6, v. 4 "And the smoke of the incense, with the prayers of the saints, ascended before God from the angel's hand."

Ps 141:1-10 (verse 2), 2 Chron 30:1-27 (verse 27), Rev 5:110 (verse 8)

Line: I came to understand that He answers our prayers with Himself.

> Luke 11:9-13, v. 13 "If you then, being evil, know how to give good gifts to your children, how much more will your heavenly Father give the Holy Spirit to those who ask Him!"
>
> Ps 28:6-9, verse 7, Ps 46:1, verse 1, Ps 78:67-72, verse 72, Ps 118:25-27, verse 27, Pr 3:21-26, verse 26 2 Cor 1:3-7, verse 3

Subtitle: Prayers From the Heart

Line: I understood our prayers must come from our heart.

> 2 Chron 6:1-42, v.29 "whatever prayer, whatever supplication is made by anyone, or by all Your people Israel, when each one knows his own burden and his own grief, and spreads out his hands to this temple"
>
> > v. 30 "then hear from heaven Your dwelling place, and forgive, and give to everyone according to all his ways, whose heart You know (for You alone know the hearts of the sons of men)"
>
> Pr 23:1-35 (verse 12)

Line: Our God is a heart God, and He is looking for us to talk to Him from our heart.

> Ps 66:16-20, v. 18 "If I regard iniquity in my heart, The Lord will not hear."
>
> Dan 10:10-20 (verse 12)

Line: I do not have the word yet to describe this, but our prayers become substances.

> Rev 5:1-10, v. 8 "Now when He had taken the scroll, the four living creatures and the twenty-four elders fell down before the Lamb, each having a harp, and golden bowls full of incense, which are the prayers of the saints."
>
> Ps 141:1-10 (verse 2), Rev 8:1-6 (verses 3-4)

Line: This is why most little children receive their request.

Mat 18:1-5, v. 4 "Therefore whoever humbles himself as this little child is the greatest in the kingdom of heaven."

Mark 10:13-16 (verse 15)

Line: He understands your heart.

Ps 139:1-6, v. 1 "O LORD, You have searched me and known me."

Mark 2:1-2 (verse 8), Luke 6:43-45 (verse 45)

Line: He only hears prayers from the heart.

Acts 10:1-8, v. 2 "a devout man and one who feared God with all his household, who gave alms generously to the people, and prayed to God always."

v. 4 "And when he observed him, he was afraid, and said, 'What is it, lord?' So he said to him, 'Your prayers and your alms have come up for a memorial before God.'"

Dan 10:10-20 (verse 12)

Line: The Holy Spirit will let you know.

John 16:5-15, v. 13 "However, when He, the Spirit of truth, has come, He will guide you into all truth; for He will not speak on His own authority, but whatever He hears He will speak; and He will tell you things to come."

John 14:15-18 (verse 17), Heb 10:11-17 (verse 15)

Line: He will also help you to pray from your heart.

Rom 8:18-30, v. 26 "Likewise the Spirit also helps in our weaknesses. For we do not know what we should pray for as we ought, but the Spirit Himself makes intercession for us with groanings which cannot be uttered."

v. 27 "Now He who searches the hearts knows what the mind of the Spirit is, because He makes intercession for the saints according to the will of God."

Line: The Holy Spirit came to help us do a lot of things the way God wants them done.

1 Cor 2:10-16, v. 11 "For what man knows the things of a man except the spirit of the man which is in him? Even so no one knows the things of God except the Spirit of God."

v. 12 "Now we have received, not the spirit of the world, but the Spirit who is from God, that we might know the things that have been freely given to us by God."

John 7:37-39 (verses 38-39) Jude 1:20-23 (verse 20)

Line: My reply to them is, "Ask Him to help you pray from your heart."

Ps 51:1-19, v. 10 "Create in me a clean heart, O God, and renew a steadfast spirit within me."

Line: After you ask Him from your heart, you do not have to ask Him again.

Mat 7:7-12, v. 11 "If you then, being evil, know how to give good gifts to your children, how much more will your Father who is in heaven give good things to those who ask Him!"

Ps 50:12-15 (verse 15), Ps 66:19-20 (verses 19-20)

Line: Now thank Him.

Phil 4:2-7, v. 6 "Be anxious for nothing, but in everything by prayer and supplication, with thanksgiving, let your requests be made known to God;"

Col 4:2-6 (verse 2)

Subtitle: Prayers Don't Have a Shelf Life

Line: Another thing I came to understand about prayer is that if it is a prayer from the heart, it does not have a shelf life.

> John 17:20-26, v. 20 "I do not pray for these alone, but also for those who will believe in Me through their word;"
>
> > v. 21 "that they all may be one, as You, Father, are in Me, and I in You; that they also may be one in Us, that the world may believe that You sent Me."
>
> Ps 102:12-22 (verse 17), Acts 10:1-8 (verse 4)

Line: He wants your loved ones to be saved more than you do.

> John 3:1-21, v. 17 "For God did not send His Son into the world to condemn the world, but that the world through Him might be saved."

Line: Remember, the Father gave his Son, Jesus, so that they could be saved.

> Rom 5:6-10, v. 8 "But God demonstrates His own love toward us, in that while we were still sinners, Christ died for us."

Line: It does not matter if you see it answered here on earth or when you are in Heaven.

> Luke 15:1-10, v. 7 "I say to you that likewise there will be more joy in heaven over one sinner who repents than over ninety-nine just persons who need no repentance."
>
> > v. 10 "Likewise, I say to you, there is joy in the presence of the angels of God over one sinner who repents."

Line: They prayed for a great, great, great, great grandchild to know Jesus as Lord and Savior.

> 2 Tim 1: 3-7, v. 5 "when I call to remembrance the genuine faith that is in you, which dwelt first in your grandmother Lois and your mother Eunice, and I am persuaded is in you also."

Line: Our prayers cause movement in the Kingdom of God. Jesus is strategizing by how we pray.

> Mat 9:35-38, v. 38 "Therefore pray the Lord of the harvest to send out laborers into His harvest."
>
> Ex 34:1-10 (verse 9), Phil 1:19-26 (verse 19)

Line: In the Bible we can read that we are to pray for the Lord to send laborers into His harvest in Matthew 9:37-38.

> Luke 10:1-12, v.3 "Then He said to them, 'The harvest truly is great, but the laborers are few; therefore pray the Lord of the harvest to send out laborers into His harvest.'"
>
> Gen 19:1-29 (verse 29)

Subtitle: Jesus Giving Out Orders

Line: Another thing that must be said loud and clear is that we have the only God who hears prayer.

> John 11:38-44, v. 41 "Then they took away the stone from the place where the dead man was lying. And Jesus lifted up His eyes and said, 'Father, I thank You that You have heard Me. '"
>
> > v.42 "And I know that You always hear Me, but because of the people who are standing by I said this, that they may believe that You sent Me."
>
> Ps 65:1-4 (verse 2), Ps 115:3-8 (verses 4-6)

Line: I saw only one God, and He was not sharing His throne with anyone else.

> John 17:1-5, v. 3 "And this is eternal life, that they may know You, the only true God, and Jesus Christ whom You have sent."
>
> 1 King 18:1-39 (verse 27), Ps 68:1-35 (verse 20)

Chapter 15 Notes

I Saw God the Father On His Throne and His Love for Us!

Subtitle: None

Line: He is the true Spirit and we must worship Him in spirit and in truth.

> John 4:1-26, v. 23 "But the hour is coming, and now is, when the true worshipers will worship the Father in spirit and truth; for the Father is seeking such to worship Him."
>
> > v. 24 "God is Spirit, and those who worship Him must worship in spirit and truth."
>
> Isa 40:27-31 (verse 28), Jer 23:16-24 (verse 24)

Line: In Heaven I heard all of creation except those who have been redeemed refer to the Father God as the WORD.

> John 1:1-5, v. 1 "In the beginning was the Word, and the Word was with God, and the Word was God."
>
> Ps 54:41, Ps 119:84-96 (verse 89)

Line: Now, those of us who are redeemed would call Him Father.

> John 20:11-18, v. 17 "Jesus said to her, 'Do not cling to Me, for I have not yet ascended to My Father; but go to My brethren and say to them, 'I am ascending to My Father and your Father, and to My God and your God.'"
>
> John 1:6-13 (verse 12), Eph 5:1-6 (verse 1)

Subtitle: What Does the Father Look Like?

Line: He is vast.

> Ps 90:1-2 , v.2 "Before the mountains were brought forth, Or ever You had formed the earth and the world, Even from everlasting to everlasting, You are God."
>
> Job 9:1-35 (verses 10-11), Ps 89:5-7 (verse 6)

Line: The angels that fly around him saying, "Holy, Holy, Holy" to Him, are very small compared to God.

> Rev 4:1-8, v. 8 "The angels that fly around him saying, 'Holy, Holy, Holy' to Him, are very small compared to God. 'Holy, holy, holy, Lord God Almighty, Who was and is and is to come!'"

Line: Or better yet, we have the form of God.

> Gen 1:24-28, v. 26 "Then God said, 'Let Us make man in Our image, according to Our likeness; let them have dominion over the fish of the sea, over the birds of the air, and over the cattle, over all the earth and over every creeping thing that creeps on the earth.""
>
> Num 23:19, 1 Sam 15:24-35 (verse 29), Rom 1:18-32 (verse 25)

Line: He is bright like Jesus with many colors coming off of Him.

> Dan 7:7-10, v. 9 "I watched till thrones were put in place, and the Ancient of Days was seated; His garment was white as snow, and the hair of His head was like pure wool. His throne was a fiery flame, Its wheels a burning fire;"
>
> Deut 33:1-2 (verse 2), Ps 18:7-15 (verse 12)

Subtitle: The Father's Throne

Line: He was sitting on the throne and yet, He is the throne.

Ps 45:1-17, v. 6" Your throne, O God, is forever and ever; A scepter of righteousness is the scepter of Your kingdom."

Rev 20:11-15 (verse 11)

Line: The throne was bright and looked like a cloud.

Ex 34:1-9, v. 5 "Now the LORD descended in the cloud and stood with him there, and proclaimed the name of the LORD."

v. 6 "And the LORD passed before him and proclaimed, "The LORD, the LORD God, merciful and gracious, longsuffering, and abounding in goodness and truth,"

Ps 68:1-35 (verses 4,33-34), 2 Chro 6:1-11 (verse 1)

Line: What I experienced about the Throne was that God the Father was and has never been separated from the Throne.

Luke 9:27-36, v. 34 "While he was saying this, a cloud came and overshadowed them; and they were fearful as they entered the cloud."

v. 35 "And a voice came out of the cloud, saying, 'This is My beloved Son. Hear Him! '"

Ex 13:21-22, Rev 15:5-8 (verse 8)

Line: I only could say to myself after seeing God on the throne, in the midst of the throne, and being the throne, "Who could make a Throne for God, but God?"

Ps 90:1-2, v. 2 "Before the mountains were brought forth, Or ever You had formed the earth and the world, Even from everlasting to everlasting, You are God."

Ps 50:12-15 (verse 12), Ps 68:32-35 (verse 35), Dan 7:11-14 (verse 13)

Subtitle: Our Father's Love for Us

Line: But out of all that I saw, what really stood out to me was the love that He has for each and every one of us on earth.

> Eph 1:3-6, v. 3" Blessed be the God and Father of our Lord Jesus Christ, who has blessed us with every spiritual blessing in the heavenly places in Christ,"
>
>> v. 4 "just as He chose us in Him before the foundation of the world, that we should be holy and without blame before Him in love,"
>
> Ps 36:6-5 (verse 5), 1 John 4:7-10 (verse 10)

Line: I came to understand that every time we take a breath of air, the Father God is saying, "I love you."

> Gen 2:1-7, v. 7 "And the LORD God formed man of the dust of the ground, and breathed into his nostrils the breath of life; and man became a living being."

Subtitle: We Are All Number One

Line: I understood that there is no number two in God's eyes.

> 1 John 3:1-3, v. 1 "Behold what manner of love the Father has bestowed on us, that we should be called children of God! Therefore the world does not know us, because it did not know Him."
>
> Ps 36:7-9 (verse 7), John 15:9-16 (verse 9)

Line: I came to know how valuable we are to Him:

> Mat 10:27-31, v. 29 "Are not two sparrows sold for a copper coin? And not one of them falls to the ground apart from your Father's will."

v. 30 “But the very hairs of your head are all numbered.”

v. 31 “Do not fear therefore; you are of
more value than many sparrows.”

Ps 33:10-12 (verse 12), Col 1:12-14 (verse 13), Rom 8:29-33 (verse 31)

Chapter 16 Notes

Worship Before the Throne of God

Subtitle: None

Line: Between them and the throne was something like water. John said in Revelation that it was like a crystal sea.

Rev 4:1-11, v. 6 “Before the throne there was a sea of glass, like crystal. And in the midst of the throne, and around the throne, were four living creatures full of eyes in front and in back”.

Rev 15:1-3 (verse 2)

Line: Just before I saw what was happening before the throne of God, all of what we would call sound, stopped.

Rev 8:1-6, v. 1 “When He opened the seventh seal, there was silence in heaven for about half an hour”.

Zech 2 :6-13 (verse 13)

Subtitle: The Heavenly Worship Leader

Line: This being seemed to be making music within itself.

> Ezek 28:13-14, v. 13 "You were in Eden, the garden of God; Every precious stone was your covering: The sardius, topaz, and diamond, Beryl, onyx, and jasper, Sapphire, turquoise, and emerald with gold. The workmanship of your timbrels and pipes…"

Subtitle: A Call to Worship

Line: It was calling all of Heaven to praise the Father and Jesus, which was this being's purpose.

> Ps 66:1-20, v. 1 "Make a joyful shout to God, all the earth!"
>
> > v. 2 "Sing out the honor of His name;
> > Make His praise glorious."
>
> Ps 108:1-6 (verse 2)

Line: I saw to the right of me and to the right of the throne, a large multitude of beings that rose up as on a number of elevators off their knees like the first being did.

> Dan 7:9-17, v. 10 "A fiery stream issued And came forth from before Him. A thousand thousands ministered to Him; Ten thousand times ten thousand stood before Him. The court was seated, and the books were opened."
>
> Rev 7:9-13 (verse 9), Rev 19:1-7 (verses 1,6)

Subtitle: The Multitude of Beings

Line: I knew that some of the heavenly beings had been there before the throne for what seemed to me, to be forever.

> Rev 4:7-11, v. 8 "The four living creatures, each having six wings, were full of eyes around and within. And they do not rest day or night, saying: "Holy, holy, holy, Lord God Almighty, Who was and is and is to come!"
>
> 1 Chron 16:7-36 (verse 36), Ps 90:1-2 (verse 2)

Line: Each being was shining and beautiful. The redeemed who had been human on earth were shining and white as light. The others were all colors and shining.

> Dan 12:1-3, v. 3 "Those who are wise shall shine like the brightness of the firmament, and those who turn many to righteousness like the stars forever and ever."
>
> Rev 19:11-16 (verse 14), Mark 9:1-12 (verse 3)

Line: This multitude started to praise the Father.

> Rev 5:8-14, v. 9 "And they sang a new song, saying: 'You are worthy to take the scroll, And to open its seals; For You were slain, And have redeemed us to God by Your blood Out of every tribe and tongue and people and nation,'"
>
> v.11 "Then I looked, and I heard the voice of many angels around the throne, the living creatures, and the elders; and the number of them was ten thousand times ten thousand, and thousands of thousands."
>
> Ps 117:1-2 (verse 1), Rev 4:10-11 (verse 11)

Line: Each song sounded so wonderful, beautiful, lovely, and so utterly indescribable with human words.

> Rev 14:1-5, v. 3 "They sang as it were a new song before the throne, before the four living creatures, and the elders; and no one could learn that song except the hundred and forty-four thousand who were redeemed from the earth."

Subtitle: The Crystal-Like Sea's Part in Worship

Line: Before these notes got to the Father, the Crystal-like Sea that was in front of the Throne, rose up in the atmosphere and intercepted the notes. Then this sea would make a hole in itself so that the notes could dance through.

> Ps 93:1-4, v. 3" The floods have lifted up, O LORD, The floods have lifted up their voice; The floods lift up their waves."
>
> > v.4 "The LORD on high is mightier Than the noise of many waters, Than the mighty waves of the sea."
>
> Rev 22:1-5 (verse 1)

Subtitle: Dancing in Heaven

Line: After the notes left the Crystal-like Sea into the atmosphere, the notes met up with the colors coming off of the Father.

> Ezek 1:1-28, v. 28 "Like the appearance of a rainbow in a cloud on a rainy day, so was the appearance of the brightness all around it. This was the appearance of the likeness of the glory of the LORD."
>
> Rev 4:1-11 (verse 3)

Subtitle: The Thunders of Heaven

Line: The atmospheres were praising the Father on the throne.

> Rev 10:1-7, v. 4 "Now when the seven thunders uttered their voices, I was about to write; but I heard a voice from heaven saying to me, 'Seal up the things which the seven thunders uttered, and do not write them'."
>
> Ps 65:7-9 (verse 8), Ps 89:5-10 (verse 5), Rev 4:1-11 (verse 5), Rev 14:1-5 (verse 2)

Subtitle: The Beings Flying Around the Father

Line: There were Living Creatures as John said in Revelations 4:6-7, 9 and seraphim as Isaiah called them in Isaiah 6:2-4.

> Rev 4:6-7, v. 9 "Whenever the living creatures give glory and honor and thanks to Him who sits on the throne, who lives forever and ever,"
>
> Isa 6:2-4 (verse 2)

Line: Some had what looked like eyes on their wings and others did not.

> Rev 4:6-8, v. 8 "The four living creatures, each having six wings, were full of eyes around and within. And they do not rest day or night, saying: "Holy, holy, holy, Lord God Almighty, Who was and is and is to come!"

Line: Within His glory, is His praise for Himself.

> Ps 24:1-10, v. 8 "Who is this King of glory? The LORD strong and mighty, The LORD mighty in battle."
>
>> v. 10 "Who is this King of glory? The LORD of hosts, He is the King of glory. Selah"
>>
>> Ex 3:13-22 (verse 14), Ps 8:1, 2 Cor 1:15-24 (verse 20), Rev 4:1-8 (verse 3)

Subtitle: The Father's Love Song

Line: This sound was God the Father singing back to each and every being giving Him praise before the Throne.

> Zeph 3:14-20, v. 17 "The LORD your God in your midst, The Mighty One, will save; He will rejoice over you with gladness, He will quiet you with His love, He will rejoice over you with singing."
>
> Job 35:10, Ps 68:33

Line: Nothing in Heaven stopped it or would think to stopping the song from reaching the targeted being.

> Ps 93:1-5, v. 4 "The LORD on high is mightier than the noise of many waters, than the mighty waves of the sea"

Subtitle: His Love Song for Us Only

Line: Love from God is being sent out to each and every person all the time and nothing can stop this love from reaching us.

> John 3:1-21, v. 16 "For God so loved the world that He gave His only begotten Son, that whoever believes in Him should not perish but have everlasting life."
>
> Ps 33:13-15 (verse 15)

Line: We can deny His love, reject His love or act like His love is not there, but He keeps sending it to us.

> John 3:1-21, v. 17 "For God did not send His Son into the world to condemn the world, but that the world through Him might be saved."

Chapter 17 Notes

God's Creation of Beings

Subtitle: None

Line: There were those who had been humans here on earth and now are among the redeemed in Heaven.

> Col 1:9-12, v. 12 "giving thanks to the Father who has qualified us to be partakers of the inheritance of the saints in the light."
>
> Heb 12:18-24 (verse 23)

Line: These beings had been on earth and had made Jesus their Lord and Savior while living on this earth.

> Heb 12:18-24, v. 23 "to the general assembly and church of the firstborn who are registered in heaven, to God the Judge of all, to the spirits of just men made perfect."
>
> Gal 3:26-28 (verse 26)

Line: They are perfect in every way, just as the Father, Jesus and Holy Spirit are perfect.

> Col 1:24-29, v. 28 "Him we preach, warning every man and teaching every man in all wisdom, that we may present every man perfect in Christ Jesus."
>
> Heb 6:1-8 (verse 1), Jam 3:2-8 (verse 4)

Line: They are right just like everything around them is right.

> Luke 9:27-36, v. 29 "As He prayed, the appearance of His face was altered, and His robe became white and glistening."
>
> > v. 30 "And behold, two men talked with Him, who were Moses and Elijah"

> v. 31 "who appeared in glory and spoke of His decease which He was about to accomplish at Jerusalem."

Ezek 3:1-27 (verse 14), 1 Peter 5:1-5 (verse 4)

Line: I saw life created.

Col 1:16 "For by Him all things were created that are in heaven and that are on earth, visible and invisible, whether thrones or dominions or principalities or powers. All things were created through Him and for Him."

Subtitle: My Family and Friends Welcome Me

Line: I saw my Grandmother Mary, Grandfather Lewis, Grandmother Ruth, Grandfather Begron, and many of my parents' brothers and sisters.

Mat 17:1-13, v. 2 "and He was transfigured before them. His face shone like the sun, and His clothes became as white as the light"

> v. 3 "And behold, Moses and Elijah appeared to them, talking with Him."

Mat 27:45-56 (verses 52-53), Luke 16:19-31 (verse 23)

Line: Every family member whom I was connected with because of the DNA inside of me was there; the DNA that God had made me out of.

2 Tim 1:3-7, v. 5 "when I call to remembrance the genuine faith that is in you, which dwelt first in your grandmother Lois and your mother Eunice, and I am persuaded is in you also."

Ps 102:23-28 (verse 28), Ps 112:1-8 (verses 1-2)

Subtitle: Family Matters Iin Heaven

Line: My family members and friends had pure love for me.

> 1 John 3:1-3, v. 3 "And everyone who has this hope in Him purifies himself, just as He is pure."

Line: This desire they had for me to be with them is the same desire we have for our love ones to live with us on earth forever.

> Rom 9:1-5, v. 3 "For I could wish that I myself were accursed from Christ for my brethren, my countrymen according to the flesh,"
>
> > v. 4 "who are Israelites, to whom pertain the adoption, the glory, the covenants, the giving of the law, the service of God, and the promises."

Line: I understood that these family members do not want to come back here to be on earth.

> Rev 19:1-10, v. 6 "And I heard, as it were, the voice of a great multitude, as the sound of many waters and as the sound of mighty thunderings, saying, 'Alleluia!' For the Lord God Omnipotent reigns!"

Line: We were never meant to be apart. That was not in God's plans for us.

> Gen 2:1-25, v. 24 "Therefore a man shall leave his father and mother and be joined to his wife, and they shall become one flesh".

Subtitle: Bring Back As Many As You Can!

Line: Jesus has sent us to our own family first. He wants us to talk with them and to pray for them.

> Ps 103:15-18, v. 17 "But the mercy of the LORD is from everlasting to everlasting On those who fear Him, And His righteousness to children's children."
>
> John 1:35-42 (verse 42)

Subtitle: What People Looked Like

Line: My family members in heaven and others who had been human beings here on earth, were shining and had pure joy.

> Rev 19:11-21, v. 14 "And the armies in heaven, clothed in fine linen, white and clean, followed Him on white horses."
>
> Isa 1:18-20 (verse 18), Isa 62:1-5 (verse 1)

Line: My family members in heaven and others who had been human beings here on earth, were shining and had pure joy.

> John 15:9-17, v. 11 "Now I am no longer in the world, but these are in the world, and I come to You. Holy Father, keep through Your name those whom You have given Me, that they may be one as We are."
>
> Ps 92:1-4 (verse 4), Jude 1:24-25 (verse 24), Rev 6:7-17 (verse 11)

Line: This shine looked like a long robe but it was really the glory of Jesus coming out of their beings.

> Rev 21:22-27, v. 23 "The city had no need of the sun or of the moon to shine in it, for the glory of God illuminated it. The Lamb is its light."
>
> > v. 24 "And the nations of those who are saved shall walk in its light, and the kings of the earth bring their glory and honor into it."
>
> Rev 7:9-17 (verse 9)

Subtitle: Are Children There?

Line: Heavenly beings do not age because there is no time in Heaven.

> John 3:1-21, v. 16 "For God so loved the world that He gave His only begotten Son, that whoever believes in Him should not perish but have everlasting life."

Mat 22:23-33 (verse 30), Mark 12:18-
27 (verse 25), John 6:22-40 (verse 40)

Subtitle: What Will We Be Doing In Heaven?

Line: Since you are there forever, you are fulfilling your purpose in Heaven.

Mat 17:1-12, v.17 "And behold, Moses and Elijah appeared to them, talking with Him."

Rev 22:6-11 (verse 9)

Line: No one was thinking that their purpose was any less than anyone else's purpose.

1 Cor 12:12-31, v. 12 "For as the body is one and has many members, but all the members of that one body, being many, are one body, so also is Christ."

Line: ...but every creation of God was serving each other.

Isa 12:12-31, v. 25 "that there should be no schism in the body, but that the members should have the same care for one another."

Line: Every creation was equal.

Rom 12:3-8, v. 5 "of whom are the fathers and from whom, according to the flesh, Christ came, who is over all, the eternally blessed God. Amen"

Chapter 18 Notes

This Is Not Our Home

Subtitle: We Are Just Passing Through

Line: It was great to really know that this was not my home.

> John 15:18-25, v. 19 "If you were of the world, the world would love its own. Yet because you are not of the world, but I chose you out of the world, therefore the world hates you."
>
> 2 Cor 4:18-5 (verse 18), 1 John 2:15-17 (verse 15)

Subtitle: This Earth is Not Our Home

Line: We are ambassadors here, we who know Jesus as Lord and Savior.

> 2 Cor 5:12-21, v. 20" Now then, we are ambassadors for Christ, as though God were pleading through us: we implore you on Christ's behalf, be reconciled to God."
>
> Eph 6:10-20 (verse 20)

Line: Today's earth is not as good as yesterday's earth and tomorrow's earth is not as good as today's.

> 1 John 2:15-19, v. 17 "And the world is passing away, and the lust of it; but he who does the will of God abides forever."
>
> Gen 3:17-19 (verses 17-18), Rom 8:20-22 (verse 21)

Line: This is a desire of all of God's creation. This is the only desire of our Savior to all of mankind.

> Rom 8:18-30, v. 22 "For we know that the whole creation groans and labors with birth pangs together until now."
>
> > v. 23 "Not only that, but we also who have the first fruits of the Spirit, even we ourselves groan within ourselves, eagerly waiting for the adoption, the redemption of our body."

Line: God Himself, wants us to know this is not our home and we are only passing through.

> John 15:18-25, v. 18 "If the world hates you, you know that it hated Me before it hated you."
>
> > v. 19 "If you were of the world, the world would love its own. Yet because you are not of the world, but I chose you out of the world, therefore the world hates you."
>
> John 18:28-38 (verse 36), 1 John 2:15-17 (verse 15)

Line: We will outlast every problem we have.

> Col 3:1-11, v. 1 "If then you were raised with Christ, seek those things which are above, where Christ is, sitting at the right hand of God."

Line: We will live on either in Heaven with God, or in Hell where everything is wrong, but we are going to have to leave.

> Phil 3:17-21, v. 19 "whose end is destruction, whose god is their belly, and whose glory is in their shame—who set their mind on earthly things"
>
> > v. 20 "For our citizenship is in heaven, from which we also eagerly wait for the Savior, the Lord Jesus Christ."
>
> John 6:22-40 (verse 40), 2 Thess 1:3-12 (verse 9)

Subtitle: The Elderly Lady

Line: I was home. I was home. I WAS HOME!

> Eph 2:1-9, v. 6 "and raised us up together, and made us sit together in the heavenly places in Christ Jesus"
>
> John 14:1-4 (verse 3)

Chapter 19 Notes

Angels

Subtitle: None

Line: We as humans like to make gods out of God's creations and angels are one of them.

> Rom 1:18-32, v. 25 "who exchanged the truth of God for the lie, and worshiped and served the creature rather than the Creator, who is blessed forever. Amen."
>
> Gal 1:18-24 (verse 18), Col 2:11-23 (verse 18)

Line: Humans like to make gods out of evil spirits, devils and demons.

> Rev 9:19-21, v. 20 "But the rest of mankind, who were not killed by these plagues, did not repent of the works of their hands, that they should not worship demons, and idols of gold, silver, brass, stone, and wood, which can neither see nor hear nor walk."
>
> Jer 10:1-6 (verses 8-9), Hos 13:1-3 (verse 2)

Line: They are made for His purpose.

> Ps 89:1-52, v. 7 "God is greatly to be feared in the assembly of the saints (Angels), And to be held in reverence by all those around Him."
>
> Mat 26,47-56 (verse 53), Mat 28:1-8 (verses 2,7)

Line: Now that you have these meanings let us look at these verses to understand that angels come in every size and shape. Some look like humans and some do not.

Rev 4:6-9, v. 7 "The first living creature was like a lion, the second living creature like a calf, the third living creature had a face like a man, and the fourth living creature was like a flying eagle."

Ezek 1:1-28 (verse 10)

Subtitle: The Horse-Like Angels

Line: There were so many horses. It was surprising to me.

Zech 1:7-10, v. 8 "I saw by night, and behold, a man riding on a red horse, and it stood among the myrtle trees in the hollow; and behind him were horses: red, sorrel, and white."

Rev 6:1-9 (verses 2,4-5,8), Rev 19:11-21 (verses 11,14,18- 19,21)

Line: And yet when you read the Bible you see in Revelation where Jesus is coming back on a white horse.

Rev 19:11-12, v. 11 "Now I saw heaven opened, and behold, a white horse. And He who sat on him was called Faithful and True, and in righteousness He judges and makes war"

v. 12 "His eyes were like a flame of fire, and on His head were many crowns. He had a name written that no one knew except Himself."

Line: There are also a red, a black, and a pale horse mentioned.

Rev 6:1-17, v. 2 "And I looked, and behold, a white horse…

v.4 "Another horse, fiery red, went out…"

v. 5 "So I looked, and behold, a black horse..."

v. 8 "So I looked, and behold, a pale horse…"

Subtitle: The Little Angels

Line: The smaller angels have just as much power as the bigger angels do because they are working under the authority of God. It is God that gives them power.

> Mat 13:34-52, v. 41 "The Son of Man will send out His angels, and they will gather out of His kingdom all things that offend, and those who practice lawlessness"
>
> Mat 13:34-52 (verses 49-50)

Subtitle: Do We Have Guardian Angels?

Line: One of the most asked questions I get is, "Do we have Guardian Angels?" The answer is yes.

> Mat 18:10-14, v. 10 "Take heed that you do not despise one of these little ones, for I say to you that in heaven their angels always see the face of My Father who is in heaven."
>
> Heb 1:3-14 (verse 14)

Line: We have more than one.

> 2 Kings 6:8-23, v. 17 "And Elisha prayed, and said, 'LORD, I pray, open his eyes that he may see.' Then the LORD opened the eyes of the young man, and he saw. And behold, the mountain was full of horses and chariots of fire all around Elisha."

Line: They are all doing what they are created to do for God in Heaven with love.

> Ps 103:20-22, v. 20 "Bless the LORD, you His angels, Who excel in strength, who do His word, Heeding the voice of His word."
>
> Dan 7:9-10 (verse 10)

Subtitle: What Do Angels Look Like?

Line: Maybe one out of four angels looked human.

> Ezek 1:1-28, v. 10 "As for the likeness of their faces, each had the face of a man; each of the four had the face of a lion on the right side, each of the four had the face of an ox on the left side, and each of the four had the face of an eagle."
>
> Rev 4:1-11 (verse 7)

Line: Angels are genderless; they only look like male or female.

> Mat 22:23-32, v. 30 "For in the resurrection they neither marry nor are given in marriage, but are like angels of God in heaven."
>
> Mark 12:24-26 (verse 25), Luke 20:35-37 (verses 35-36)

Line: There are angels that look like light, fire, water, air, clouds, wind, trees, and flowers.

> Luke 24:1-8, v. 4 "And it happened, as they were greatly perplexed about this, that behold, two men stood by them in shining garments."

Line: There are angels that look like light, fire, water, air, clouds, wind, trees, and flowers.

> Heb 1:5-14, v. 7 "And of the angels He says: 'Who makes His angels spirits and His ministers, a flame of fire?'"
>
> 2 King 2:2-18 (verse 11) Isa 6:1-3 (verse 2) seraphim means: burning one

Line: So for now know that there are more angels that stayed with God than went with Satan.

> Rev 12:7-12, v. 9 "So the great dragon was cast out, that serpent of old, called the Devil and Satan, who deceives the whole world; he was cast to the earth, and his angels were cast out with him."

Line: I end this chapter with this—we are only to worship God (Father, Son, Holy Spirit), and not angels.

> Rev 5:1-14, v. 11 "Then I looked, and I heard the voice of many angels around the throne, the living creatures, and the elders; and the number of them was ten thousand times ten thousand, and thousands of thousands,"
>
> v. 12 "saying with a loud voice: 'Worthy is the Lamb who was slain to receive power and riches and wisdom, and strength and honor and glory and blessing!'"

Chapter 20 Notes

Eight Things I Was Told About The End of the Age

Subtitle: These Eight Things Will Take Place to Signal the End of the Age!

Line: EVERY NATION IS HERE FOR THE PURPOSE OF GOD!

> Job 12:23-25, v. 23 "He makes nations great, and destroys them; He enlarges nations, and guides them."
>
> Dan 4:13-18 (verse 17), Dan 4:23-25 (verse 25)

Line: KINGS AND QUEENS, OR WHAT YOU CALL PRESIDENTS AND PRIME MINISTERS, ARE ALL PUT IN POWER FOR THE PURPOSE OF GOD!

> Rev 17:12-18, v. 17 "For God has put it into their hearts to fulfill His purpose, to be of one mind, and to give their kingdom to the beast, until the words of God are fulfilled."
>
> Dan 2:20-23 (verse 21)

Line: MORE, EVERYDAY, SONS AND DAUGHTERS OF GOD WILL BE PLACED IN RULERSHIP OF NATIONS FOR THE PURPOSE OF GOD!

> Job 36:7 "He does not withdraw His eyes from the righteous; But they are on the throne with kings, For He has seated them forever, And they are exalted."
>
> Job 34:29-30 (verse 30)

Line: RAISING PEOPLE FROM THE DEAD WILL BE COMMON IN THE LAST DAYS OF THE AGE!

> Luke 7:11-17, v. 14 "Then He came and touched the open coffin, and those who carried him stood still. And He said, 'Young man, I say to you, arise'"
>
>> v.15 "So he who was dead sat up and began to speak. And He presented him to his mother."
>
> Mat 9:18-26 (verses 24-25), John 11:1-44 (verses 43-44)

Line: GOD IS NOT WORKING THROUGH ONE PERSON, BUT THROUGH HIS SONS AND DAUGHTERS IN THE PRESENT AGE. STOP PEOPLE FROM CHASING MEN, BUT HAVE THEM FOLLOW GOD!

> Titus 1:10-16, v. 10 "For there are many insubordinate, both idle talkers and deceivers, especially those of the circumcision,"
>
>> v.11 "whose mouths must be stopped, who subvert whole households, teaching things which they ought not, for the sake of dishonest gain."

Line: THE GOOD NEWS OF GOD IS NOT FOR SALE AND HE IS GOING TO STOP THE SELLING OF IT BY HAVING MORE GIVE WHAT THEY KNOW AWAY. FREELY IT HAS BEEN GIVEN AND FREELY THEY MUST GIVE!

> Mat 10:5-15, v. 8 "Heal the sick, cleanse the lepers, raise the dead, cast out demons. Freely you have received, freely give"
>
> > v. 9 "Provide neither gold nor silver nor copper in your money belts."
>
> Jer 23:1-8 (verse 2), 1 Tim 6:3-10 (verse 3)

Line: THAT WHICH IS EVIL WILL LOOK GOOD, EVEN TO THE SONS AND DAUGHTERS OF GOD. THE SONS AND DAUGHTERS OF GOD WILL GROW IN PRAYER IN THAT TIME AND NEW EYES WILL OPEN, SPIRITUAL EYES. THEY WILL SEE FROM THE HEART!

> Mark 13:3-13, v. 5 "And Jesus, answering them, began to say: 'Take heed that no one deceives you.'"
>
> > v. 6 "For many will come in My name, saying, 'I am He,' and will deceive many."
>
> Isa 30:8-11-13 (verse 10), Eph 1:15-21 (verse 18)

Line: VISUAL DECEPTION WILL INCREASE IN ALL AREAS OF THE WORLD!

> 2 Thess 2:1-11, v. 9 "The coming of the lawless one is according to the working of Satan, with all power, signs, and lying wonders,"
>
> > v. 10 "and with all unrighteous deception among those who perish, because they did not receive the love of the truth, that they might be saved."
>
> Mat 6:22-23 (verse 22), Heb 3:7-15 (verse 13)